Heartily Yours

By

Susie Bell

**Blog Writer of
www.heartilymindful.com**

This book is a perfect expression of the depth of feelings experienced by sufferers of mental health issues. It's a voice of comfort and understanding at a time when the loneliness engulfs you…...Trudi mental health sufferer

Copyright to Susan Bell

My books are protected by international copyright laws. You are not, however, authorized to sell, trade, republish, or create derivative works based on any of my books (nor any portion thereof, including book covers) in any format, for any purpose, without first receiving my express written permission. Any violations will be prosecuted upon detection in accordance with international copyright laws.

Acknowledgements

First person to thank is Roger and happy birthday, my rock, my human angel and a lot more you will hear him being called throughout this book. For the past 8 months he has stood by me through thick and thin, he has talked to me, held me, loved me and most of all encouraged me with my depression, blog and book, he has sat whilst helping to care for his mum and getting better from his own breakdown editing and collating my book whilst I have been at work. He has heard so many times whilst making dinner or before going out, 'hang on I have to post this first!' Thank you beautiful, I do not know what I would do without you, I love you so much, always have and always will.

The next to thank is my friend Julie, my best friend for 27 years, stood together, lost each other and found each other again, nothing ever changed except we both grew up, and love each other more and are very close, with and without talking, she has helped me by being there and talking through things, reading my blog and sharing it around when she read it. Thank you Julie for being my rock when Roger was ill, Love you loads always will.

Other friends to thank for standing by me, with this blog, book and my depression, just by talking, June, Jane, Kara and Ruth, thank you all so much for accepting me as I am and helping me to getting where I am today with Roger and myself, I couldn't have done it even though you have your own lives to live and things going on. Thank you all four of you, love you all.

I would like to say a very quick thank you to my Elefriends on www.elefriends.org.uk you have all supported me along with a lot of Facebook Pages and Twitter friends. Thank you all lots of hugs it has meant a lot.

Preface
Written By: Sara Breidenstein;
Owner and Author of Kissing Stigma Goodbye

It is estimated that in any given year, mental illness affects 1 in 4 people! Wow, 25% of individuals live with a mental illness every year! You may not have realized the number was that high; many don't. This could be the case, partially because a large majority of individuals do not openly discuss their mental illness for fear of judgment. This could also be partially because many people are just not educated on all aspects of mental illness from what the symptoms are to the statistics related to it, and all other things mental illness related. Despite being part of 25% percent of the population, many individuals living with a mental illness live every day feeling alone and ashamed for having a mental illness; avoiding discussing their mental illness for fear of judgment and non-acceptance by others. These feelings of loneliness, fearfulness, shame, judgment, etc. originate from the stigma that society has placed on individuals living with a mental illness.

As defined by Webster's Dictionary; stigma is a mark of shame or discredit. Stigma is real and stigma hurts. Society places a burdensome stigma on individuals living with mental illness. This stigma does not come without a variety of negative consequences for the individuals in which it is placed upon. Individuals living with a mental illness face this type of stigma on a daily basis, in one form or another which is quite detrimental to the mental health and the overall well-being of those individuals.

Stigma causes individuals living with a mental illness to feel shameful and therefore causes many to live in silence and fear. Stigma can steer individuals away from receiving the necessary treatment due to feelings of shame and embarrassment. Why should anyone ever feel shamed for having a mental illness? It is not a choice, it is an illness, something one is born with. Society does not typically make individuals feel shameful for having a physical illness of any sort; society is caring and nurturing, offering help to the individual or the family in those cases. Realistically speaking, no one should ever feel shamed or at fault for having any illness, mental illness included. Additionally, no one should feel scared or ashamed to receive treatment for their mental illness; stigma gets in the way of appropriate and timely treatment. Stigma is extremely hurtful and damaging to individuals living with a mental illness and can have long term negative effects on individuals.

I personally was diagnosed with Bipolar Disorder 14 years ago. I have faced stigma first-hand more times than I can count over the years. As a result of stigma, I have historically found myself extremely ashamed of the fact that I have a mental illness. I never told anyone that I have Bipolar Disorder unless I absolutely had to. I even found myself not being completely honest with my Psychiatrist for fear of judgment, which kept me from receiving the proper medications to treat my symptoms. Last year, I finally found myself able to begin to break free from the stigma, fear, and shame that had been holding me back for so many years. I began to tell my story and beautiful things started happening. For one, I began to feel a sense of freedom I had never before felt. Secondly, I was also able to connect with individuals all from all over the place that I never would have connected with otherwise. I began receiving messages from individuals, all with a common theme. That theme was individuals thanking me for sharing my story and for providing them with a place where they felt a sense of belonging and comfort to speak about their illness. Individuals living with a mental illness are looking for a place to feel like they belong; they are looking for a story that says "you are not alone". Many of us don't ask for much; we just ask to feel accepted and not alone.

How do we break free from this stigma? What can we do to fight it? How can we help individuals living with a mental illness feel belonging? Susie Bell has done a great job at doing just that for so many individuals living with a mental illness. Her blog titled Heartily Mindful is an amazing portrayal of what life with mental illness is like; she has provided a place where individuals living with a mental illness can find a sense of belonging in a welcoming, heartfelt environment. Susie has told her story in a way that is informative and helpful to others; to individuals living with a mental illness as well as individuals who are not affected by a mental illness daily. Education is vital to ending stigma. Most stigmatic thoughts and actions come from a lack of knowledge or education, not a deliberate act of hatefulness. Heartily Yours compiles Susie Bell's blog of honest, encouraging and real life stories from the heart; portraying her struggle with mental illness. She aims to be of help to others living with a mental illness as well as part of the fight to get rid of the stigma surrounding mental illness.

Many don't realize the extreme importance of a book like Heartily Yours. However, those living with a mental illness will never forget the huge impact that finally feeling a sense of belonging has had on their lives and on their recovery. Without individuals telling their story we will never reach awareness. Without awareness we will never get rid of stigma. While stigma remains, individuals living with a mental illness will never feel a sense of peace and belonging in this world. Standing up and telling ones story of life with mental illness is not easy; it is very brave and it could save a life. A book like Heartily Yours is nothing short of empowering!

"If someone listens, or stretches out a hand, or whispers a word of encouragement, or attempts to understand a lonely person, extraordinary things begin to happen."
Loretta Girzartis

Prologue

If I could let you into a secret of why I wrote this book and start my blog www.heartilymindful.com please do not laugh, because there are many things in this life to laugh at, however Mental Health Illness is not one of them, that doesn't mean we can't laugh though.

Mental Health is something that has been kept in the dark for far too long or pushed away to a hole so that it is hidden, which is why so many of us are so scared of saying anything to anyone about having something like Depression or Bipolar.

I have had Depression on and off for over 20 years, this is the first year I have had someone to stand by me and really understand what I am going through, not just for the reason that he has had his own mental breakdown, I supported him through it until I got to the stage I could no longer hold it all together, I was carrying too much, needing help with support as well.

For me mine has been slightly easier, because some of Roger's friends are helping me through this as well as standing by Roger at the same time, I have been able to talk about things that have hit me and knocked me right down.

Why, I wrote this book, because I wanted to tell you the reader whether you have or do not have a Mental Health Illness what it is like to go through a day of either work, sick or days of holiday what it is like to live with a Mental Illness.

Trying to help employers realise that we can be employed if only there was someone there to help listen to our problems for just five minutes and for those of you who work around us to sit and hear how we really fell for five minutes and not to leave us in the cold, to help us to join in with things. We are human beings as well, we aren't moody, we just need to focus and concentrate a little harder at times, so we are a little quieter, help us to join in, don't laugh at us.

I had so much to say to a lot of people, I want to end the stigma by taking a brick from out of my wall, making the first hole, by telling you what goes through my mind each day, the struggle to get out of bed, but, having work has helped.

Having Roger to support me and talk to me, you wouldn't know what a difference it has made, to let me be me, to not say "Snap out of it". I don't know where I would be if it hadn't been for him or his family and friends, he encouraged me even when I was down hearted to keep going, that I was good at it, that people were hearing what I have said.

If you read all my poems you will see some of them have a certain darkness and sometime they will then skip up, this is what depression or any mental illness is like.

To be encouraging before you start reading I would like to end by saying that I have been told and I still have yet to have faith and confidence as any Mental Health sufferer does in myself, that I have been inspirational and caring.

Heartily Mindful - my blog name means written from the heart and feelings of the mind, please after reading my book visit my blog, the next book will be as good, every step I have taken either forward or backwards is in this book, but, if you see any frightening images of yourself in these poems see someone and talk perhaps to your doctor or a friend first.

My name is Susie Bell I am 42 Years old, I write for my blog www.heartilymindful.com please join me with my blog daily or read the books as they are published so we can stand together and united to end Mental Health stigma by telling everyone we are normal we are not our illnesses, we just have an illness hidden inside

Monday, 1st April 2013 - Welcome

Welcome!

This is a blog of the heart and the mind for anybody to join in. I am going to attempt to write a poem a day to stop the stigma that anyone with any kind of mental health issues cannot help themselves or others by speaking to them through their own problems.

I have been on a few forums and put my poems on one or two which brought me to writing my own blog with a poem a day, please join in, comment, criticize or add your own if you wish anything that will help others to get through what they are going through.

Thank you very much for joining

Welcome - Heartily Mindful

Today I am doing something I have never done before
Something that has been tried many others
I am going to try this another way
I want those around me to look around them
To see what having mental health problems means

It means you are as normal as them
You and I are human
We still look the same
We may not think the same
I wanted to step out of my comfort zone

I want to help myself
I want to shout from the rooftops
That we need help
We need to talk
We aren't stupid just because we have problems

We all have mental health problems once in our lifetime
We just need to shout to other people
We need to write as we don't know how to say it
You will see poems from me
Poems that are about mental health

The mental health problems are from the heart
Because I am there and my partner is coming out of it
I know what it is like
I want to help others by reaching out to them
I also want to stop the stigma and laughter of mental health

It isn't funny, but, we can laugh
We are wanting to be normal like the others around us
We keep turning, hearing and seeing their lives
We will get there

Monday, 1st April 2013 - Courage

This poem lifted myself, a couple of readers and I hope it lifts you as well :-

It takes courage to walk in others shoes
Courage if you don't think you have any in the first place
To do what you need to get on with life
I know a lot of people with a lot more courage than me
Courage comes from the heart

It takes courage to publicly open myself up
Courage taken with someone stood with me
Courage to ask someone for help
To know who to ask
Courage is not just for lions

Courage comes from the mind as well
You have to think what you are going to do next
Courage comes from small things
Then it takes larger steps onto bigger things
Try Courage it feels good

It doesn't matter what courage is
Courage is life in general
To carry on when you think it's not worth it
When you think that nothing is going right
Courage comes from deep within

Courage is there in every step you take
To me courage can be in the small things
Courage doesn't have to mean the large things
You are having courage to listen to me now
I am having courage to write

Monday, 1st April 2013 - Please

Please listen to me
Hear what I have to say
It may not be very nice
You can judge me later
Or you can just ignore me I really don't care

That is me I don't care
I just want you to know
Know that I am not straight
Not straight mentally
Listen or ignore me I don't care

There are thoughts racing through my head
They won't stay still
I can't stay still
I get really happy and then more often than not
As low as not wanting to be here

There is only one person
That's stop me from doing anything stupid
This is the first time I have taken the first step
The first step to realising that I am not just low
That this could be for life

I don't want the person who is standing by me to go through it
He has got so much on his plate already to add me would just hurt
I'm scared and have been scared for many years
To even think about this
To realise that I am the major problem in my life not anyone else

I wanted to say this out loud
I wanted to be understood by people who understand
I know what I do, I know how I think, I also know it is what it is
I have to keep going because I love someone so much
Please can someone answer me and tell me I'm wrong.

Tuesday, 2nd April 2013 - Beautiful Day

Beautiful day

No matter how you feel
No matter where you are
No matter who you are
No matter how dark it is for you
It is a beautiful day

They don't come along very often
You can look from under the duvet
You can peek from out of the darkness
You may feel the cold
Despite that it is a beautiful day

You can see the sunshine
It may not make you feel better
It may comfort you to sit in the sunlight
Where you can feel it's warmth
You really cannot disagree it is a beautiful day

Reach for that sunshine
Reach for the fluffy clouds around it
Reach for the blue sky
Come on now
It is a beautiful day and you have to agree

I may not be at my best
But the sun has certainly filled the blue sky
The clouds floating some of the darkness away
The wind blowing a breeze
IT IS A BEAUTIFUL DAY!!

Wednesday, 3rd April 2013 - Dark Clouds

I can tell you I do know about this, I have supported my partner through his depression and now he is supporting me through mine no matter how awkward I'm being and boy you would know it:-

The dark clouds are covering the sky again
As we settle down for the night
Each of us settling to someone different
Or even a night alone

Even those with someone can feel lonely
Loneliness is not a good feeling
It is a lost feeling
Like you are watching everyone through a goldfish bowl

When you see through the bowl
Everyone is talking and you are calling
Slapping the glass
Not being heard

Keep shouting, keep tapping
You will be heard
You will be seen
Someone will see you need help

Then it is up to you to take it
It may be a hand
It may be a loaned ear
It may even be a shoulder to cry on

When you shout loud enough
When they hear you
You have to let them help you
First of all it is up to you

When you have had that help
find someone to talk to
Someone you may be able to help
I have now

I have been there
I have been in that goldfish bowl looking outwards
I tapped, I asked for help
I am getting help from the person I helped

All I can say is talking does work it doesn't matter who or where
Have a good evening! Remember to talk

Thursday, 4th April 2013 - First it starts with you

This I feel is so right to be said, if we want to change something it starts with yourself, if we want to take stigmatism away from depression and other mental health conditions it has to start with us talking about it, writing about it, singing about. As my title says it starts with you and only you, make a difference which I hope I am:-

First it starts with you

Do you want change
How do you want change
When do you want change
Why do you want change

Change starts with you
Change starts when you want it to
Change starts for a reason
But most of all you have to be ready for that change

Last year I had to change
Why?
Because I was so unhappy
Because there was no way of changing that unhappiness

My time had come to change
I walked out of my home
With the things that I owned no joint possessions
It took several weeks

I had help to make that change
I had been in depression asking for no help all year
I knew that as soon as I made this change
My life was going to turn upside down, I did it

I had to make the change
I wanted to make the change
I needed to make the change
Yes, I may have swung into another depression

I know that this depression is different
I will come out of it for good
I have the support from someone who I have supported
Someone who helped me make the change

The change you make will be for the better
It is for me
I know it may not seem it
I have been able to help someone survive what I have been through

This is how I can explain so much
This is why I can tell you change is good
But, only you can start that change
Start it whenever you can

When you do start that change
Talk to someone as I am you
Help someone else make the change
Help them realise that only they can make the change

Your life is yours
You want to forget
If you forget what you have been through
You won't help someone survive

I know if it wasn't for the change I made
I wouldn't be here on earth
I wouldn't be able to write about coming out the other side
Survival is change

Change is your life
Make a difference to someone elses life
Be an ear, a shoulder, a comfort, a friend
Shed a tear, shout, scream or even talk
Let it out, let it change your life

Only YOU can start the change!!

Friday, 5th April 2013 - Scared

These are my feelings at the moment for those of you who think that I am not where you are, I am and I keep going there, not just after the counsellor, please read I'm not just a machine, I am a human being too :-

Scared

I feel scared
Scared that people don't want to hear me
I feel like the cloud floating in the sky
Not the ones that have been out today
A grey cloud, the one inside my head

That cloud is just floating by life
Life that everyone is enjoying
The life that seems to be there
But not

I am crying for help
But no-one can help
I can hear what's in my head
But, I can't talk about
Because it is messed up

Messed up like my whole life in general
I know I have someone to talk to
But he can't hear me
I keep knocking, but I can't come in
He has enough on his plate

I know that I should talk to someone
But I can't
There is no-one else
I wish I didn't feel so lost
I wish I could be strong

I just feel so far away
I am trying to hold back the tears
I only want to sit in the corner
Keep quiet
I want life to go away

I know it won't
I also know that I have to stand by my man
Let my problems be nothing
Let them be the smaller again
Here they come the tears

I am now feeling sorry for myself
The cloud is raining
How much longer can I go on like this
I go to work with a painted smile
Then come home with tears in my eyes

It won't be long
Won't be long before what
Before I talk to a counsellor
When did a counsellor do any good
They did and then after 6 weeks they say goodbye

Guess what, everything I needed hasn't been resolved
So I carry on and then after a while start again.
Start going back down hill
Start watching life feeling like nothing
Feeling as though I should never have been born

I want to make a difference to someone's life
I want to help someone else
I can't like this
I want to talk to someone

Saturday, 6th April 2013 - Help For All of Us

I wish that I could help a lot more
I wish that I could do a lot more
All I can think about is how to write
Write in poems to others

Reach out and help you with experience

You may or will have more experience
The one thing I will say is that I am added help
If I am the start to your help, thank you

What I want to do is to be able to take away
"Depression" you, and the laughing
Either by colleagues, friends, or employers
You want them to believe we all have to live normally

Hold your head up high
Smile when needed
Talk to someone
Someone who wants to talk, who will understand

Someone who doesn't care what you are feeling
As long as you can do the work
As long as you are still wanting to work
And as long as you come into work

If I can touch just one person
One person to help someone else
I know that I will have done something to help
Through my own depression, through my own mental health problems

Please talk to someone, someone who needs help
Talk within work take the stigmatism away
Raise a discussion within the workplace
Help someone who may be going through the same as you

Someone who is crying because they have to paint that smile on
Someone who is hiding and cringing at their desk
Because they find it hard to talk to someone from work
Not only will you help that person and you, but help to take away the stigmatism

One day it will be alright to walk into work with a mental health condition
I have one, I have to work
I have talked to someone
Boy, it helped

Let's take this stigmatism away, it will take time, we will all do it!!

Saturday, 6th April - Time

I don't have all the answers in fact I may not have any at all, but, I know that if we try the first step then we will get there. I know for some of us it isn't easy, that the corner, the duvet, goldfish bowl, grey clouds and other adjectives to describe depression or our mental health has been with us for way too long, and that the clouds where you reside aren't going to be the same as outside my window, envisage it even if you can do that it is a step inside your head to get out of it, time will help you with the rest.

It does take time, little steps and a little bit of courage, just reading this today is taking the courage, picturing this inside your head is courage. There are some of you who ask 'How do I know what I'm talking about?' If you read my other poems on this blog you will understand I have been in and and out of my own grey cloud for over 20 years always wanting to be the last time. Please read this poem and best wishes to you all speak to you again tomorrow - Heartily Mindful

Time

Feel the breeze of the spring wind
Feel the warmth of the summer sun
Hear the call of the mating birds
Hear the sounds of the World

Walk away into the wondering crowd
Stand up tall to be counted among them
Put your hands in your coat pockets to warm them
Now you are walking among them

Let the hum of their talking ring in your ears
Don't let it disturb you
Listen to them talking and smile
Smile because today is your first day

The first day you stepped out
Take a look around you it is a whole new world
For you that is
But there is something different

Instead of rain all the time
Instead of the grey clouds that have been hanging around
There is sun
And Mr Blue sky

The white fluffy clouds are there
You wish you could reach up and touch them
You have taken your first step
The first step from that goldfish bowl

The goldfish bowl that every 3 seconds stays the same
The corner of the room you have been crying in
For hours, days, months, years or even decades
You have finally put your head outside the window

The window which was left open by someone
Someone who cares, who knows how you are feeling
Who wants you back
They may not be someone you know

They are looking down on you still
They left that window open
They wanted you to see what was out there
To see things without the grey cloud

They want you to see what they see
Now is the time to sit down outside in a cafe
Order that drink you have always wanted
Relax and take in the sun

It doesn't matter how cold it is because you are wrapped up warm
You aren't being part of the crowd and on your own
Someone sits with you realising you're not mad
You say hello

The first hello you have said to anyone
You have been scared
There is no need to be now
They just want to talk

Talk about anything it doesn't matter
It will stop you thinking about that dark cloud
It will help you off load that dark corner
What you don't know is they are reaching to help you

What they don't know is what you have been through
You are talking to someone
You have a smile on your face
The sun in your eyes, the breeze through your hair and most of all your life

Can you feel it
Can you feel the summer coming
You are going to enjoy it
You have had the courage, a little bit of strength and
You have taken the first small step on a long, busy and winding pavement

That pavement will bring you back to the World again
The same pavement will enable you to talk and shout to others
The very same pavement runs under others helping them back
Most of all you will walk alongside them and meet new people supporting them

This is the last time you walk this pavement
You will help others on the way
You will tell others about what you have been through
Go on take more time to walk some more and save someone else

Take them somewhere to stop them from going where you have been
Take their hand
Talk to them
Time will help you as long you let it

Sunday, 7th April 2013 - Change in Life

My life last year changed, it changed for the better, You are asking me how can I still be in a depression if that was the reason? because I didn't give myself time to take everything in, everything I was doing, I never took stock of my life and help myself out of the depression I was already in. I thought it would change with just doing what I had done it didn't - please read my other poems I may not have said it fully, but....One day I will, this one is for where I am today in this changed life :-

I have walked
I have ran
I have glided
I am drifting

What all these movements are for
I am unsure
I know it was for one thing
That was to change my life

My life changed
Now I am drifting around
One day my feet will be on solid ground
They will stay still

For now though
I will keep floating around
As the thoughts do in my head
As the clouds do up above me

I have something to hold onto
I have a steady rock
I have a smile
I have tears

Most of all I can write
This is the thing keeping me going
This is the work that keeps me floating
It is my rock and my hope

My life may have changed
But, I am free
Free from the bars that once held me
The rings that bound me

My heart beats
Beats a different rhythm
My life changed
To be here, which is good

Monday, 8th April 2013 - Help Me

Please join me and others to talk about mental health as if it was a cold not something to be ashamed about hear me and help all those around you :-

HELP ME

Please tell me if you are
Mindful of others
You listen to others
You treat others as you would like to be treated
Or do you just sit in silence

Please tell me
Would you like others to be mindful of you
Would you want others to listen and hear you
Would you like others treat you like everyone else
Or do you just sit in silence

If you sit in silence
Nobody will take any notice
You won't be heard and others to listen
You won't be treated like everyone else
So don't sit in silence

You don't have to
Be brightly dressed to be noticed, just stand up and be counted
To be heard or listened to you need to talk or maybe shout
Be treated as an outsider you are part of this World
Please don't sit in silence

What can happen
Is for you look up and stand up
You can be heard or listened to
You can be treated as a normal person
You won't sit in silence

You will
Notice others to help you be noticed
Hear and listen to others to be heard
Treat others as normal so that you can be treated as normal
This will help you and others stop the silence of depression or mental health

The tears will fall
The pain won't go away quickly
The feeling of despair will slowly go
You have helped you and reached out to others
Most of all you will join together to make this silence a thing of the past

I have another that I want to share with you, I know it is a lot to have two in one day, but, this way I can tell you another bit about myself:-

Me

I cry my tears in silence
Sometimes just in my heart
I feel the pain and agony
The darkness that hangs over me
This time it has been a very dark tunnel

It is a time I won't forget
Because the time has been too long
I have gone through so much
So much hurt, upset and change
Never knowing where I am

Time where I needed to stop and think about things
I have had to keep going
Not allowing myself to stop
I am still keeping going
I have to or I won't know how to start again

My world just keeps spinning
I want to forget the past, I can't
There is just too much there to forget
It is like the dark corner that I hide in
It is the dark cloud hanging over my head

I know that at this moment in time
I can help someone
I can talk to someone
Reach out to someone
Even if it is through my writing

Dry the tears
Put the light on
Look at the sun
The future is ahead
This is how I try to talk to myself

Try it.

Tuesday, 9th April 2013 - Where have you gone..What have you done?

Well, short and sweet as this is where I am today

Dear Me
Where have you gone?
I just want you back
I'm struggling without you
I want that bright bubbly person

Dear I
What have you done with me?
I want that new person back in my life
The bright woman who made such major changes
I'm just painting that smile with tears inside

Dear Myself
Are you in there?
Have you seen yourself
Have you watched yourself go down hill
Do you think there was anything that could have stopped this

Dear All of Me
Yes, you could have talked
I know what I look like, I can see inside
I want to shake me and shake me
You will come back the bright, bubbly person

Dear You
It will take time, a lot or a little time
You need to keep talking
You will need to take steps
Steps to get you there
One day you will get there, you will be you

Look to the future Me
There is a bright, intelligent young lady
The beauty inside and out goes without saying
Then you can live again, not struggle with the now and past
You can help someone else, now you've helped yourself

Wednesday 10th April - Talking to a stranger

I thought you would like to hear what a stranger, a nice stranger did for me yesterday the emotions it raised and the reason why, you see she had told me that I had been suppressing my depression until now, what I have been doing for 37 years, now I have someone to help me and support me to get better, someone who wants me, someone who themselves have been through the same, if you try talking to a stranger or a friend you will never know what happens:-

I stood last night in the kitchen
Holding a drink
I cried, I shouted, I screamed, I got angry
This was at someone, someone I love
I was pushing them away

I was hurting because for the first time
I talked, I had spoken to my counsellor
What was scary? Why was I crying or angry?
Because she summed me up in 45 minutes
What I had been living in 37 years

She had realised what had happened
She said that she would help me
She told me to carry on with this writing
With helping others around me
If this is the one thing that helps me, it gets my thoughts out.

Most of all I want to say sorry to the one I love
I would like to say thank you for reading this
I would like to say I did calm down enough to put a poem on here
To comfort my loved one with his pain
This is me, I look out for others whilst helping myself

I want you to stop and think what you could do
It only has to be the smallest of thing
Say hello to a sad person
You never know what you can do with just one word
You may get a smile

Talking to others isn't easy
Not when you are in a low mood
Try it, you never know
It may help you as well
Reach out and touch someone today

Thursday 11th April - Life's Path

My mind and brain has so much to say and in very many different ways, excited, sad, joyful and anxious about what is going through my head, I am hoping this makes sense and you will find it as uplifting as I did writing it:-

Life's Path

Life has a path for you
A path that may not be so smooth
So straight, or even so bright
There may even be some walls

There are going to be a lot of crossroads
Some you will have to make hard decisions
Some will be easy
But if you keep steady you will get there

The walls around those paths
Are to help you stay on it they bend where you bend
They will go where you choose to go
What makes it all the fun are the people those walls let in

They will let them in and then they may let them out
But, there are some that will stay
Whichever the case they are the people
The people who have helped form your life

They have given you some good times
And sometimes we all wish to forget
Most of all they have formed your here and now
You can still look back, but you must always look forward

The pathway is long
It is formed by the choices which we make
The people whom we meet
The journey that we take at each crossroads

The only person that will always be there is you
You will be travelling
It will be an adventure for you to take
You never stand still

It doesn't matter how you are feeling inside
Each second changes the path you take
Each second puts another choice in front of us
What we need to do is get the courage to get up and do that challenge

The challenge is life itself
The minute ticks by, the hours turn another hand

The hours turn to days
Those days help us along

Now you are weary take a sleep
Look at what and who is around you
Dream of the path being smoother
That day will come when you have overcome your obstacle

When you can see what is ahead
When you can hear the people with you
I know what is ahead
The future, it looks bright for you or I

Friday, 12th April 2013 - My Body

My heart beats on the wings of the dove
So high above the clouds
As free as the wind
As hard as the rock that I stand on
Even faster every day

My eyes are as open as the sky above
With tears that sometimes flow
They close as tight at night as the door behind me
They see all around them as an eagle
They watch even more each day

My head is full like the clouds fill the sky
Full of memories like a fast moving photograph
Full of thought like a jotter full of notes
Full of people I want to remember
I remember these things always

My limbs are strong like the sun lighting up the sky
Having peeled back each layer like an onion
Having carried things like an elephant
Having held people I love in them
They have helped me change my life

All of these are held by one thing my body
My body is perfectly shaped to help these
It has been held to help with a lot of these things
It has to be strong enough
I know it is and it will help me take every movement

Friday, 12th April 2013 - Yourself in the mirror

Stop!
Give me two minutes
Two minutes to ask you
Ask you why you are rushing around

Calm down!
Take a deep breath
Talk to me
What's the hurry?

Chill!
Now breathe out
Look around you
Do you see why you need to chill

Relax!
See what is actually around you
See who is here
Doesn't that feel good

Now if you hadn't stopped
If you hadn't chilled
Hadn't relaxed
You wouldn't be able to find the time

Find the time to say hello
Time to say goodbye
Time to see what is staring you in the mirror
Yourself.

Friday 12th April 2013 - Live Life

I can see the sunshine on a rainy day, can you? I can see the path stretched out in front of me, I can see the future, it may not be very clear at the moment, but, I know that I have one, try looking around you, listening to your thoughts and hearing them for yourself, the tears will flow for those choices, they may be difficult they may be easy most of all though it is you who has made them, no-one else.

Live Life

Throw your arms in the air as if you don't care
Smile like you have never smiled before
Jump up and down as if you are a mad bunny
Laugh right from the soul of your body
Because you are here and alive

The snow has turned to rain
The rain turned to clouds
The clouds turned to sunshine
And the sun is shining brightly in the blue sky
Because you are here and alive

Your stony field has turned to a stony mud
The stony mud has turned to a stony pathway
The stony pathway has turned to smooth
Your smooth pathway to straight, but choiceful pathway
Because you are here and alive

You are here and alive
As anyone else is on this earth
Everyone has these choices
Everyone takes their own chances
We are all here to live

We all have memories and people we choose to forget along the way
We have the times we may want to forget
Most of all we have choices we wished to forget
Along with the places we want to forget
We know that all of these have made us what we are

Now you have heard me or the people around
Listen to yourself
Someone you may have not heard that much before
What do you want in your life
Where do you want your path to go

What way do you want your path to go
Only you can make that choice
So with life in your body, sun shining on you and your path stretched out in front of you
What are you going to do?
I know what I want to carry on doing and I will listen to myself
Live my life the way I want to not the way anyone else wants me to!!!!

Saturday, 13th April 2013 - Rowing Life's Stream

Slowly I row myself up the river
I watch the flowers and the trees around me
As I splash and row with my oars
The river is still and calm as I think

I hear the birds singing in the trees
With the bees buzzing in the flowers
The animals are wondering through the grass
The trees bowing over the silent water

The fishes dancing in and out
Whilst the people quietly pass me by on the banks
As I row
I smile to think what a beautiful world

Watch the world go by in a transe
Watch nature grow around me
Smelling the fresh air, the scent of the flowers
There is a place, a place to stop

A peaceful place to stop
To think about the things that I have seen
Things that I have seen around me
When I sit and look around I am able to think about all the things that have happened to me

Saturday, 13th April 2013 - Peeling back the layers

I have watched myself peeling back the layers over the years and never learning from it, now though, I am starting to learn how it helps me to be with others, how each layer in some way means something to me, how I can look at the people I used to be with and the family I love, learning that life gave me each layer to learn from:-

Peel back each layer
Think about peeling an onion
Each layer is different
Think about them as an experience of your life

Each one has it's own route
It's own home
It's own distinct flavour
They are all different in their own way

If you sit and think about each of them
In which way it has got you to where you are now
It has helped you with the course of life you are on
You should ask yourself would you be where you are now

After sitting and thinking about them
Thank them, it doesn't have to be in person
I know I do every day
For they have changed your life to what you are and what you are going to be

You can move on to great things
If you haven't already.
My life has got better, but
I am still waiting to come to terms with others as do you

It will happen, just remember the good
Keep hold of what your changes are now
So you can pass it on and help someone
Someone who may need help or so you don't go back again

The layers that we have peeled back
The paths that we have all taken
The people we have met
Are all for a reason, that we are who we are today

We have memories
We have learnt things
So that we can be stronger people
So that we can help those if we need it

Peel back the layers as you sit alone
Think about the memories from each one
Think about the people from each one
Reach the inner you and reach out to someone to be able to help each other

Saturday 13th April 2013 - A Thank You

I have added a new post today, because I feel that instead of putting this in my older poems I need to share this, because I feel it is so appropriate for so many people, you may not believe, but, how many do say Oh My God, thanking him or praying to him secretly without knowing it. This is not a religion out reach I know that when you read this poem you will know how right I am :-

Oh My God
I know I don't talk to you much
But you have obviously helped me with the changes in my life
You have walked with me as I prayed to change it
You have given me what I have got today, Thank you

Oh My god
You have given me so much in the past 12 months
You have given me friends
You have given me a man I love and loves me
You have given me time to think, Thank you

Oh My God
My life had been in torment for so long
Now it seems to be unravelling towards the good
Somewhere I can see my future without the haze
What you have given me is my life back, Thank you

The tears have rolled
The anger has shouted
The time is healing the wounds
The strength will soon be there
Thank you for helping me back to my own two feet

Thank you for answering my prayers and not giving up on me.

Sunday 14th April 2013 - What have I done?

I don't think I have to say much that my poem doesn't already, except ask the question. "What have you done in your life?" post a comment at the bottom : -

What have I done in life
I have sat here and thought and thought about it
When I get asked what are you or who are you
I sit and think about it

What have I done in life
I have looked back over life to see many changes
Changes over the years that have helped
Some changes that have hurt

What have I done in life
I know now though having thought about them all
I have been many things, I have done many things
Some things I am pleased to have done and others not so

What is so different
The changes I made to please were the ones that made me happy
The others that aren't so have done everything to drag me down
I have fought to get back up on my feet again

What is so different
The things that weren't good are the things that have made me stronger
They have made me fight
But, they have never let me forget

What is so different
I can't forget those things, I have kept hold of them
I have kept hold of them to remember how I coped
How I can get out of it when I have to again.

What has happened
I have been through life's twists and turns
This time I am determined I am going to stay out of it
Because I know I will never need to use them again

What has happened
I am determined that I am going to use what I have been through to help
I have helped someone who is becoming stronger
A strength that is now holding me together and I love him for that

What has happened
I have passed on my strength to this person
In time I will get it back again, we will stand tall, smiling and happy
We will help others as we have helped each other remembering

What else
There isn't much else except one thing
Remember the good times, the good people and good memories in your life
They have helped me through

What else
Talk to someone, it doesn't matter who
Talking is good, it is a relief to finally realise that someone wants to hear
Someone cares, it doesn't matter if they are close or a stranger

What else
Talk, you never know what happens
Try a smile at least one a day
Live, live life you only have one chance to live it.

Now
I am going to try to help put strength into me
I am going to love the man who loves me
Most of all I am going to live life with him as my strength

Now
It is your turn, remember the good times and the bad
turn the bad into times to be thankful for
Thank the family and friends who have changed your life

Now
All you are going to do is stand up straight
Smile just once a day
And think about what I have said.

How do you cope? Tell me who you are?

Sunday, 14th April 2013 - My Heart will go on

I wanted to add this piece to thank a very special someone in my life for whom I wouldn't be here if I wasn't for him, it is a little soppy for those who want to turn away do :-

My heart will go on
Not only will it go on, it is only for one person
A person who has given me such courage
Such bravery to carry on with life

How do I know we are meant to be
Because there is so much that we have been through
So much that we are going to go through
We have both had strength for each other in tough times

When were those tough times
They are just finishing now for him
There will be some more ahead for me
What we know is we will get through it

I know that this man doesn't care about what I am like now
He just wants to help me get to being me.
It is what I want and I am so determined this time
I have someone who understands, and knows what it is like

We will never give up for as long as the sun shines
I have loved him from the day we first met
He has supported me as a friend
He is my bestfriend

He looks as me as though there is nothing around me
He has the most beautiful face
He is the most beautiful person in my life
He is sexy and most of all loves me

I know that every day I keep thanking him for choosing me
For letting his heart open to me and hold me
I feel so special when I am out with him
I feel so special when he holds me in his arms

Thank you for supporting me and your strength to be a better person.
My man, friend, best friend and my life, I love you xxxxx

Monday, 15th April 2013 - Different Places...different minds

I walk through the jungle
Walking in between the entangled branches
The entangled vines
With the leaves that have fallen on the floor
And the ones that take away the sunlight from my face

I remember how dark my life has been and is now
I may have a lot of good things going around me
But a lot of the time the bad overcasts the good
I find myself taking steps back to think about all that has happened

I have found hills that seem like mountains to climb
Ones that I don't feel that I would ever get to the top with
I listen to all around me and there is nothing, silence
The clouds hovering over me white and fluffy

I watch the sea come turning in and the waves crashing against the rocks
Just like the angriness deep down inside me
For all the stupid things I have done in my life
Then I stop to think about how these stupid things that have got me where I am

All these journeys and views have certain places in my mind at the moment
Some are calming
Some are sad and some are of anger
I would say that there are others in same minds
All I can say is thinking and talking will certainly help to soothe these places for you

Tuesday, 16th April 2013 - Just One Day

The wind is blowing through the trees
As the flowers glow brightly in the sun
The birds singing brightly in the blue sky
With me sat down here watching it all

I clear my head enough to do some thinking
Even though I need to do some talking
There is nobody around
They are all sleeping

Sleep?
I wish I knew what that was
Even having a chance to doze
When all I can do is think
Think about times and people gone by

Each thought I have is one I don't want
It has been tainted by someone or something
As the leaves rustle their sound trying to take me away
Away from the thoughts

The beautiful colourful flowers dance in front of me
Trying to get my attention
To think nicer things
To enjoy the peace and tranquillity instead of the black cloud

As the bird duck and dive
I start to watch the beautiful blue sky
Watching the dance of the butterfly
Smile, because I can think those things later

The black cloud has gone for today
Hopefully it won't come back until I can speak to someone
Someone who will listen
One day, just not today

Wednesday, 17th April 2013 - Lift The Wall...Help Someone Understand

I am writing about one situation not necessarily yours because every situation is different and not everyone is able to do this, I am plucking out of mid air how perhaps I should tell my manager. Not everyone has someone to tell this to, but, just listen to it, imagine you are in front of someone and talking to someone when reading this it doesn't matter who, someone who doesn't know what you are going through:-

Good evening, how are you?
I don't know, I think to myself
I want to tell you that I'm feeling low
I want to tell you I have a mental health problem
I just don't know what you would say

I want to tell you that my mental health problem is
It is....IT IS DEPRESSION
Blast, you seem to be shocked, you thought I was normal
Now you have gone quiet
You don't know what to say, of all the people......

Don't do that?
Do what you ask
Walk on egg shells, I am still me
I have some hard things to resolve, demons to get rid of
I don't want you to think of me as any different to be with or to talk to

Tell me about it, you say
It isn't easy
Go on help me understand, you ask
There may be times when I feel normal
That doesn't mean I am better

Carry on, you ask, don't stop or hold back
There is a cloud, it could be all colours white, grey, very grey or black
Or another way as I can see I need the explain
It is like walking through a very thick forest
You are at the edge, walk into the darker part and you could be at the lowest edge

But, you start, I thought that you couldn't work or do anything
As I said I look normal on the outside, I try to do the norm
I want to keep going, I have to keep going
If I stop I start thinking about bad things, the things I have to think about to make me better
I have to do it to stop me from thinking about harming myself

Do you want me to keep going?
You nod your head; it looks like you are ashamed
Ashamed that you had never really thought about asking how I am
When I come to work with you or for you
You think that I am alright, you didn't realise that I have come to work with depression

I have been working with you for a while
I want to tell you, to show you that I am working through things
Both personally and with work
I am as normal as anyone else except I have a mental health problem as anyone has in their life
I can laugh with people, I can smile at people, I can have a joke
When I get home, I sit and talk to other people

As I finish work, this is the edge of the forest
As I drive home, the forest gets darker
I know though when I go home
I have someone to help and support me
Someone to talk to me, talk things through

That someone is a person who will hold me if I am low
Someone who will be there even when the times are good
I need to have a structure, I needed to tell you
I don't want anyone treating me any less normal than the next person
I want to work, to know I am able to join other people and work.

So what happens if you are low at work? you ask
Just do the same as you would with anyone else
Talk to me or leave me alone, normal
All I ask is not to walk on eggshells
I leave it up to you what you want to do now I have opened up

You hang your head and shake it
I wouldn't have known
No, I answer, I was ashamed to tell you
I now know that this is nothing to be ashamed of
I want people to realise that depression is real and I no longer want to be silent

Thursday, 18th April 2013 - Stop!!!

I didn't listen to anybody, not my own mind when I was too busy, it took my body to tell me I needed to or had to slow down, I have been ill since the beginning of the year with infection after infection, fighting depression all because my body was telling me to stop and I didn't listen until I turned very poorly with all the infections and even having to go to hospital. What I am asking you today is to stop and take the time to listen to you and hear your thoughts:-

Stop!!!
I want you to listen
What can you hear
Your heavy breathing
Your heart beating
Silence of voices around you

Because you are being drowned
Drowned in a pond of darkness
You haven't given yourself time
Time to help yourself relax
To let yourself think

To let the thoughts run through your head
Like a babbling brook
Instead of getting to the stage where you just have a cloud
To think easily and calmly
Not like a train running through a station

To let your body rest peacefully
Watch the trees blow in the breeze
As you sit and think, relax
Chill out
Do you want to turn into a volcano
Ready to erupt at any time

Live your life looking forward
Take each day at a time
Plan, not making everything such a rush
Take it steady
You need time

Don't stop when you suddenly explode
Asking the World to stop turning
Not when you feel as though you don't want to go on
Stop! Now!
Before the cloud grabs you and keeps you in its clutches

Friday, 19th April 2013 - Deep Inside

I am sat here in a dark room, I've been writing poetry for as long as I can remember. My life has changed for as long as I can remember. I have struggled with depression throughout my life. I have only just realised over the last few months that I can use my creative writing, poetry or verse to help myself and others. So I would like to share with you my passion tonight:-

Somewhere deep inside
Inside yourself
Inside your heart
Inside your head
Is a passion to be you

A passion that could be you
A passion to do something to help you be you
Something that could be anything
You should feel it stirring
If you can, then keep the thought going

The thought could be the one thing
That one positive thing to keep you going
To push away even the smallest part of negativity
The negativity that has been clouding
The real you

Dig deep and find it
Find the old feeling
Even find the new feeling
Look ahead with what you can do
So that part of the dark side moves away

Do be disappointed if that part
The part of the black cloud does come back
You have to work at it staying away.
It can only stay away if you want it to
Keep the new feeling the new passion going

I know it will be difficult
I know how hard it is
That is why I'm here
Writing every day
Keeping my passion going to help my black cloud

Friday, 19th April 2013 - Tracks of tears

Another for today:-

Track the tears of my heart
It is crying out to speak to you
To tell you how I feel
To tell you what I feel
Feelings you can't understand or don't know about

I have sat in a corner waiting to burst
I have cried a lot of tears
I have seen the sun come and go
I have seen you pass by
I have seen crowds of people but can't hear them

I can hear my own voice screaming in my head
I can feel the tears because they won't stop
I can feel the cold wind blow
When the cloud hovers above me
Because I can't feel the warmth of the sun

I feel the pain
But the tears won't heal
I can feel the hurt of all that I went through
And the cloud just keeps hiding it
The smile I wear is not always real

My tears are making a pool
As I watch them try to soak into the ground
Trying to stop them from falling
Trying to think about something good
Something that is deep down

Deep down inside
I am trying to find the positive thing
The passion I have inside
Which is why I am writing tonight this late
Because my heart has cried

My heart and head have been covered by a black cloud
One which I didn't feel like I was going to get out of
Even the person who supports me couldn't help
So I sat back here again
Working at my passion, poetry

Saturday, 20th April 2013 - Calm and Peaceful

Well as you can see I have had a beautiful day, but, you can take this poem in whichever context you want to either with the weather or with what is happening for yourself today, I know that I am not exactly smiling, but, I have had a good day. I hope you have too and enjoy the evening as I will be with my new family, enjoy this poem as I have writing it :-

What a calm and peaceful day
A day full of beauty
A day full of silence
A day which is held in my heart

What a beautiful and silent day
A day doing the garden
Planting trees
Planting new seeds

What a day to remember
Sitting in the warm spring sunshine
Only a very slight breeze
With not a grey cloud in sight

The day is too nice
Too nice to spoil
A way to walk without the forest around
A time to take stock of the rest of the year

A way to keep me happy
Pottering in the garden as I sit
Sit in the garden watching the breeze and sun dry the clothes
Air through my mind blowing the cobwebs away

I think that today is a good day
If you have been doing as I have sitting enjoying the sun
I will later on open a beer and drink to today.
I give thanks to whomever for this wonderful today having spent it with my new family

Saturday, 20th April 2013 - Peace and Serenity Hand in Hand

To follow on or add to my first post is this poem, please make sure that you read the other one as well, because they fit together:-

Peace and Serenity
Did you ever think about how it would feel
Do you know what it is like
I have always thought about it as my own piece of heaven
If there is such a thing

Take a look around and see if you can see it
See peace and serenity hand in hand with nature
Hand in hand with life
Hand in hand with everything around you
Watch the sky, the sea, the mountains, the hills and fields

When you watch the sky
The colours it changes to at different times of day as your mood does
The way the clouds float away without a care
The way the weather changes quietly
Just like your life, peacefully though

When you see and hear the sea
The waves crashing against the rocks
Which feels like the anger inside your heart, and your head
The spray that comes up to your face to cool you
The sea is full of wondrous life, like you

When you look at the mountains
The snowy white peaks so peaceful and calm
The greyness of the stone underneath feeling embracing tranquillity
Like the layering within your life
The layering of your days and how you feel

When you walk the green hills
The grass growing under your feet
The flowers blowing in the wind and against your face
Feeling like you can touch the sky as you get higher
Hearing the silence of the peace around it

Walking through the fields in the wheat
Feeling the ears of corn flicking against your hand
Can you feel it
The wind is whistling through it
I can feel the peace and serenity as I hear nothing around me

The noise of the crowd has disappeared
The noise in my head has silenced for just a few moments
To allow me the time to take a break
Only for a short moment
This one time for peace and serenity to go hand in hand to think about these things

Saturday, 20th April 2013 - Me

As you can see I am on a roll and enjoying my passion, especially with trying to lift the stigmatism for depression and mental health:-

You don't think I know where you've been
You don't think I have cried those tears
You don't think that the anger is almost bursting
You don't think that I feel out of control of my life
That I just sit here writing these things

I am here, crying on a good day
Crying the tears that can't be seen
Wanting to know why I am having to take things I don't want to
Trying to find the answers running through my head
Why my thoughts can go from good to bad in just a snap

Why I can feel myself starting to slip away
Why I can feel that cloud coming over my head
What control can I keep over my life
None, because of all the things in the past
I don't always take my advice

I do talk
I do think
I try to think and do positive
What I want to do and what I do
They are two different things sometimes

I want my voice heard
I don't want sympathy
I want to tell you is I am a human as anybody walking this planet
I want to be treated as anyone else does
I have a right

You see I can get angry, I can also push away
I can push the one I love away as well
I am lucky he still stands with me
I know that I am also determined
I mean determined to come out of the other end for good

If I do I will not stop writing
It will be happier
Also I will not forget what I have done
To help others come through their bad times
Be it permanently or temporarily.

Heartily Mindful is who I am
Wanting to tell and help others with experience
It doesn't matter who you are
I am only a working woman with a man by her side
I also have depression and am not ashamed to say it.

Saturday, 20th April 2013 - Broken Glass

Now, you are going to ask if I really have got a life of my own? Yes, I have just felt like writing, try it put pen to paper. It doesn't matter who is reading, do you know what I don't care, I am able to put my fingers to the keyboard and type, it is up to you. I was scared too, scared of what people know about my depression, you may look at my poetry and think it is rubbish, do you know what I don't care, it is helping me, if it is helping others or lifting the stigmatism of mental health then I am even more pleased because I am helping others whilst helping myself:-

As I walk on this long road
A road that is twisting and turning in front of me
There is a road left behind me that is shattered
Shattered like glass shards lying on the ground
My feet are slowly healing

As I step slowly along this new road
I can still feel the shards of glass in my feet
What I do know is that
I will gain the strength to take a shard out
It will be painful, but, what good thing isn't

For every good thing that will happen
Each pain will go away
So will each piece of glass
My past will become whole

With those steps forward will also be steps back
That won't smash the glass again
It will only make things painful
I know also that it will make my future better
Myself the stronger person

As I step along each stone of the new road
I will have people helping me in each step
I have pushed and I have pulled hoping
Hoping that these sharp pieces of glass would just leave
Leave me without any pain

I should have known better
I should have known the pain would have to be there
The pain of the past to help me
Help me get past it all
All of the pain to help walk through my future

I can see my future with a bright light
I know though, to enable me to talk about my past
I have to heal and take away the pain
I can say thank you to those who helped my past to my now future
I can say it was good to have done what I did

I wouldn't be here
I also have people to thank in the here and now
As they are helping me towards that future
I have my family to thank, but, they have also caused me pain
For them to be in my future I have take out the largest shard of glass

I am now on solid ground with a little pain
A little guidance
The glass is behind me, I only have firm ground in front
I have a rock holding me by my side
You will get through this as I have with steps, small ones.

One step forward, two steps back, you and I will both get there.

Sunday, 21st April 2013 - A Fresh New Day

I haven't much to say to this as I think what I say in the poem is all I need to say, thoughtful reading and see where it leads perhaps to a fresh new day?:-

I have been walking through pastures new
Through pastures green
Where skies are blue
And clouds are white
Where the hills just ramble out of sight

I have been talking into the day
Through the minutes
Through the hours
Into the night
With a friend that's old and one that's new

I have been sleeping on and off
Through the dreams
Through the nightmares
Through the darkness into the light
Waking up without a start into the day

I have watched the dawn arise
With the early light
The sun bringing in the the new day
A bright and breezy day
Bringing a fresh new start for each of us

As the day opens up with the dawn
Birds singing from trees opening their leaves
Brightly or dull coloured flowers that make up the World
Each blade of grass that grows
Letting each animal including us to walk through nature

As each animal walks through each pathway
Each pathway will grow again
And each field will have it's season to start anew
The farmer will be able to plant each seed
Bringing a fresh outlook to each new season

Each new season, ahhh
Starts with each new month
Starts with each new week
Starts with each new day
Where you and I will start again if we let ourselves

Start each new day
With a fresh new thought
A positive thought
Each new thought
Could lead to a new way of life for you or I

Let's just sit
Sit and think about how our the first of this poem
Could affect our lives
Take a walk, take a look around open our eyes
To help start what I hope will be our fresh new life

Monday, 22nd April 2013 - A World Beyond This

You may or may not want to read this today, but, this is my day today and the poem my head wants to write:

There is a World beyond this
Beyond pain and hurt
Beyond what went on in the past
Beyond who was in my past

There is a World in front of me
A new fresh one
I just wish someone could show it me
After the day I have had, I am begging anyone to show me

My head has been fuzzy
Yet, I have still been able to work through it
I needed to finish work
So I could get home and cry quietly to myself

No, this isn't my greatest day
I know that this is for my own good
That before the end of the week
I will feel better than this

There will be a time
I can jump up and down
I will be able to say that I worked through all of these bad bits
That I am finally strong enough to smash it

I have smashed the glass ceiling
The one that seems to be getting closer and closer to my head
I knew that it could only get worse
Until it got better

I know it will get better
Just someone tell me when
Baby steps I get told
You've taken the first, I get told

My head doesn't feel like it
I am trying to stop feeling like this
Even whilst sat here talking to you
I am determined that this isn't going to beat me

I am going to beat it
I am going to beat depression
I am in a good place now
I just need to get rid of the bad parts of my life

I know I have to be thankful for what has shaped my past
I know that I have to be thankful for the people who have helped shaped my future
I just want to get rid of them now
So I can think clearly again about where I am going.

Tuesday, 23rd April 2013 - A Door

Walking through a door can be difficult for anyone:-

I am walking through a door
A hole in the wall
Which could lead to anywhere
Could lead me to anything

I am flying up above
As I hear the birds singing
The water babbling
The animals moving around

I am swimming
Through the open seas
Where their waves crash against rocks
And the fishes are swimming with me

I am moving around on the Earth
Where I am unsure of what I am doing
What is going to happen next
One minute I feel secure and then the next I don't

I know my pathway like many of yours
Will be hard and you will feel how I feel above
It will always be difficult
Eventually we will get there

Eventually there will be sunshine
After the dark cloud that hides us
There will be a light at the end of the tunnel
And we will swim rather than drowning

The one thing I will say is we have to give life another chance

Wednesday, 24th April 2013 - What, Where, How and Why?

Being that stronger person can take time as I know, I was once and I am now back on the ground read my poem and answer the questions if you want:-

Where did you go
What did you do
Have you heard
Did you listen
What is it that you know

Why is it so dark in here
When will I see
Did you speak
Do you want what
What can you tell me

Which way to go
What road to take
Why the stones
Did you see that
What are you doing

What happened
Why do I feel like this
When will it go away
What time will it come back
What day is it

I will only find this out if I come out of the forest
If I come out from the thick of it
Just peek my head around the corner
I may hear, see or speak to someone
Perhaps I may find where I am going

I may not know what day it is
I will soon find out what the time is
I feel the touch of someone
Someone who wants to support me
Someone who wants to help me find my way

The stones on the pathway are there for a reason
They are there for every pain I have had
Everytime one pain goes, one stone will be gone
I will never forget the memory just lose the pain
The memories are my life, they have made me what I am

There are people in my life I don't want to hear
I don't want to see, I don't want to know
They maybe family, they may be friends, but, they made my life
I am what I am today, I may have to let them go
No matter what, I am a stronger person because of it, because of them

The strength I have in my head
The strength in my heart
Is going to help me be the better and stronger person
To answer all the questions above
Hopefully, it will you too, if you stop and think about it.

Thursday, 25th April 2013 - One Step Forward, Two Back

I would like to know why this is taking me so far back, why I can't seem to forget so easily:-

Why do I have to step backwards
To step forward
Why can't I just keep walking forwards
Why do I have to keep stopping
In order for my life to get straight

Why can't I be like others around me
Why can't my life be straightforward
What in my lifetime have I ever done
To walk back and forth
To shed the tears I am shedding

Why am I so scared of myself
So scared of being alone
I can be independent, but, not alone
Why have these people done this to me
What do I do to get rid of these shackles around my limbs

When can I become me again
What does it take to walk back into my life again
How does everything go past me
I am missing so much
I am missing so many different people

I want to be able to be me
I want to live my dream
I want to feel the sunshine on my face drying my tears
I want the wind to blow through my hair

Thursday, 25th April 2013 -- I have a dream

I was thinking about this poem in my car this morning, why wasn't it my first post, because I wanted you to see what my day was like, now I want you to see how I feel:-

I have a dream
A dream of which
I am walking along a beautiful golden sandy beach
A dream where the sea is lapping at my feet

I have a dream
Where the skies are blue
The breeze is warm
The sun is shining down
A dream where everything is calm

I have a dream
Where the beach is quiet
There is nobody on it except me
As I walk the beach I see my steps in the sand
There is only one set of footprints

I have a dream
Where I see someone walking beside me
Someone who loves me
Someone with the strength to hold me
That someone whispers to me

I have a dream
Where the past doesn't matter anymore
Where I have left everything behind
Where the pain is behind me
And my life in front of me

I have a dream
That I will be able to look back without the pain
I will be able to thank the people who have shaped me
The me who is going to face the future
A new future

I have a dream
That I will be able to leave those people behind
Because I know I have a new one
A new future with the person who is holding me
Who is standing in my shadow

I have a dream
The person who is in my shadow
Will come out, he is and will be my future
I see us standing together
I hear the whispering from him

I have a dream
I see the sand
I feel the sea and the breeze
I hear the sounds
I feel the sun shining on my face to dry my tears

Thursday, 25th April 2013 - Barbed Wire Past

This is my last and final one I promise, I want you tell you about my barbed wire and how amazing the someone I have supporting me

Going beyond the past
Is like walking through a field of sunflowers
Even though you can't see the light
You will the height of those flowers
Will start to get shorter

The past for me
Has been hard it has been like barbed wire
Which has cut me to shreds
It has held onto my heart
But my heart was the first to break free

I am still tied up
The spikes are slowly coming out
And I have had to say good bye
Good bye to people in my past
Knowing still that they have made me what I am today

Today is and will always be a hard day
The memory will start to fade
Slowly as I take the steps to learn how to forget
Forget a day like this
A day full of memories I want to forget

I also know that my heart
Now belongs to someone else
So does my future
But they are patiently supporting me
By talking and holding when it is needed

Someone who is willing to standby me
Take time to encourage me
To see me grow
They have watched me come down
Now they want to watch me climb back up

That someone will be there when this day is forgotten
One day we will have a day of our own
One day we will both have a life of our own
One day we will be able to stand and face the future
                                        Face the future together

Friday, 26th April 2013 - A Brave New World

Take my hand, I want you to see what I would like to show you, this will not be the first tonight or this weekend, because I want you to see what I see, what I hope, a brave new world

Take a walk with me
A walk down memory Lane
A lane to you and I that can be painful
A lane where the walls have been built
A lane where there are glass houses

The memory lane we walk down
Has a lot of shattered dreams
A lot of people who now mean nothing to us
A lot of times where those people have ran out on us
A lot of times where they have just got in the way

The shattered dreams
Where promises have been broken
The good times turned to bad
There has been a stoney way
Where every stone stumbled upon I wanted to throw

Now I have my forward thinking dreams
Where I want the people of my past to be ghosts
Where the walls on the path are being taken down
Brick by brick
Each brick that's taken will be carefully laid down

Carefully laid down to make my future
By laying each one in front of me
Making my road to my new dream
Where the trees will blow in the wind
Where the flowers are brightly coloured

That is what I have missed
The colour in my life
Now, each step slowly, we can start again
Each baby step will be a step to a new beginning
A step on the long road ahead of us

The shattered dreams and promises
The people who have stood in our way
The glass houses around us
The walls that have stood in our way
They are no longer there, a brave new step

A brave new world
Take my hand now
I will help you
I will support you
                        As you support me to this brave new world

Friday, 26th April 2013 - A Change

Make a difference in this World by changing your life first, then try helping someone else who may need help, see how it makes you feel and what a difference it could make to them :-

A new day
A new step
A new way
A new thought
A new life

How to change it
How to change the way of doing things
Change towards a different way
A way out of unhappiness
It isn't easy

Easy is not life
Nobody says anything is easy
It isn't quick
You have to take one step at a time
Very little steps, A new step

Each new step
In a new direction
Will help to ease the pain
Will help ease the unhappiness
I didn't say it would be automatically

It could take minutes
It could take hours
It could take days
It could take weeks
It could take months even years

Each step we take is a fresh start
A fresh move out of the darkness into the light
From the negative to the positive
The difference between now to then
Between the past and the new future

The new future that you and I have set out in front of us
One that any of us can have
Just take that first step
The first step towards a new life

A change in the way YOU do things
If that one change doesn't change things
Make another, then another
Soon you start to make a difference
Let alone see a difference
Even a smile

When you smile
The World will smile with you
You never know who you might be able touch
You never know what a difference you will make to somebody else
Someone who hasn't been able to read this

Smile, talk and make a difference
Talk, reach out
You may never forget
You will help someone else
Someone who needs a difference

Friday, 26th April 2013 - My Dream

I know this one is a little soft for me for this time of night what do you expect: -

My dream
To be standing on a very quiet beach
There are only a few people around me
People I know

My dream
Standing on that beach in beautiful sandals
With a beautiful dress
A beautiful dress that blows around the legs of my dress with the warm breeze

My dream
For the man of my life to be stood next to me
Where he has been all this time
Holding my hand

My dream
To be walking along the beach with a smile
A smile so big
That this is what I have wanted all my life

My dream
To be finally walking in the sunshine
For there to be nobody except those who accept me for what I am
For whom I have become

My dream
To be free
To live my own life
With the one person that matters, the one who has supported me

Saturday, 27th April 2013 - A New Chance

This is only a short poem for me, but a truly meaningful one, one in which I have to learn to love myself for my past as well as what I am becoming for my future:-

As I start to make the new step
As I take a peek ahead of me
I can see the door opening slightly
I have started that change
Have you?

A new home
This was the start of my life change
New friends around my new home
I made that change
Did you?

A new man
This was the next step into my life
Someone who stood by me for me
Not someone waiting around for me to get better
Would you?

A new family
This was a big part new people
People who have become my friends
Friends who accepted me for my past
Will you?

With all this change
I have to learn to accept myself and my past
To be able to love me once again
To be able to live my new life carefree
Will you?

Saturday, 27th April 2013 - One Change

I made that one change today, I did gardening, I have never been a good or keen gardener, but, I stood and learnt today and started to change my life:-

One change, one difference, makes one new step made
Doesn't it feel good to make that one change
The one change you thought you would never make
It doesn't matter what it is
Taking a walk in the bright sunshine

One difference makes one step made, one change
If you make that one change it could make that one difference
A difference that can change your life
It could make that one step easier
Like that walk into the sunshine

Making one new step made, one change, one difference
Take that step doesn't matter how small into positive
The one positive that may change your life even just slightly
It could make the difference in your head
Take a small step into the sunshine to take that walk

It doesn't matter how long all of these take
Do it today
Make the change, the difference, take that first step
It will make you feel so good
It will be an achievement, be proud of that first step no matter how small

Take my hand
I walk you out to the first step
Take my ear
I will hear you talk about it
Be proud, you were the first to make the change for your life

Sunday, 28th April 2013 - Admittance

I know how hard this poem is because I have been through it myself. I am still having to admit to family members and find how hard it is :-

Scared?
Have you asked yourself why?
Is it because you don't know how you are feeling
Because you do, but don't want to admit it
Why not?

Afraid?
Of what?
Of knowing that you are unwell in the head not the body
Of admitting why you are feeling like this
Why can't you?

Frightened?
Sat in the corner
Tears running down your face at any opportunity, for no reason
Not wanting to talk to anyone about this
For what reason

These are the three questions that ran through my head
When I first realised what was happening
I had held back for so long not admitting to myself
Let alone admitting to anyone else
For what reason

I didn't want to admit I was ill again
I was scared, low, unhappy and holding on
Holding on to help someone else get better
Before they could be the strength I needed

Now, I have admitted it
I took the first step towards changing my life
It may only be a small step
But, for what others may seem normal to me is a step
Because I am always watching over my shoulder

I have depression
I have a mental illness
This first step I took was a strength
There is no weakness in admitting you have a mental illness
In fact it is a strength, because you want to make the first step

The first step in Depression
To talk to someone to make yourself better
If you keep hiding in the corner nothing will change
It starts with you
You aren't the only one, there are others
That is why there is help to give you

When you ask for that help
It will be given to you
I realised that after I admitted it
Now they are helping me and I am helping myself
By talking to you, to try and help you see what you are missing

It is difficult and believe me I know
If you don't do it, who will
Someone wants to talk to you
You want to talk to someone
That someone may have been where you are now

Sit with a group of people
Talk to them, ask them
You may find just one person to talk to about it
Someone who has been there or is there.
Reach out and someone will reach back to you

All I can say is admit it to yourself first and then make the change

Sunday, 28th April 2013 - Hold My Hand

I don't think there are enough ways for me to say that you have to be the one who changes, realise that there are people waiting to help, you just have to be the first to make that step, to say "Help" someone is waiting to listen to it today, if not for yourself, for those who are around you:-

Hold my hand let me take you there
Take you to where I have been and where I am
I have walked a long and winding pathway
Through a place a lonely place

I have been through the maddening crowd
Where it is noisy with the hustle and bustle
Where all I want is quiet
All I can hear is buzzing

I have been walking through fields
Fields of tall grass where the bees and birds fly by
Where all I want is to hear someone call my name
All I can hear is nothing

I have been swimming through waters
Raging waters which crash against the rocks
When all I want to do is swim through calm
All I can hear is loud noise of anger

I have been sitting in the corner
Where it is dark and gloomy
Where all I can feel are tears
All I want to do is smile

I have run into a dark forest
Where it is too quiet
I can hear the trees rustling
All I want is to feel someone touch me

I have ran up a mountain
I have shouted and not been heard
I can hear are the echoes of my own voice
All I want is my voice to be heard

I am sat in a room
I am talking, but feel like no-one is listening
I can cry, but this doesn't work
All I want is for someone to listen to me

One day the above will happen
I have to be the first to say I need help
Unless I ask they don't know
I have to be the first one to take the step

Sunday, 28th April 2013 - Walk, Think and Watch

Let the breeze blow away your grey cloud and come with me to where the sun is shining:-

Taking a walk in the sunshine
It doesn't matter where
It doesn't matter what time
It doesn't even matter how long for
Just walk

Stretch my legs
Stretch my mind
Think without the four walls surrounding me
Think with a beautiful day around me
Just think

Watch nature around me
See the butterflies on the flowers
The birds flying in the sky
The bees buzzing around
Just watch

Come with me down sunshine lane
To walk
To Think
To Watch
And blow the cobwebs away

Monday, 29th April 2013 - Talk

Talk to someone, you never know how it will help, whether it will help them or yourself:-

Listen to what is being said
Someone wants to talk to you
Hear what they are saying
It doesn't matter what they are telling you
They are talking to you

Someone wants to talk to you
They want to help you
It is difficult to hear them I know
They are wanting to help you
They want to reach out to you

Talk to people
There are a lot of them out there
Hear what they have to say
Put your point across
Shout if you have to

You know that you want to really
You do
You want to hear what they have to say
And you want to be heard
Scream if you need to, whatever is in your head

Talking to one person you are sat next to
Someone maybe feeling the same way as you
Someone who needs to talk about something
It may help you as well as them
You may give help and may be able to take help

Find someone who looks as lonely as you do
You never know what you may find
Someone to talk to or someone to help
When you have come out of what you are in
Don't forget it, you never know when you may be able to help someone else

Tuesday, 30th April 2013 - Never walk alone

I have come to the last day of my first month, this is the first month of many and I hope you keep hearing me, some poems you will like some not so, but, most of all join in write with me add your poems to my comments and I will publish them. I am helping me as well as walking with you, it is amazing how many people don't know who I am or what we are all going through, you aren't alone, you will never be alone for as long as you want me to write for you :-

Look at me
Look at my face
See where my tears have rolled
See my lips
Look at the smile

Touch my fingertips
with yours
Hold my hand with yours
We will walk this road together
Trust me I won't leave you

Talk to me
My ears are open
I want to hear what you have to say
I would like to support you
I would like my shoulders to be broad

My shoulders are there
To be cried upon
I will show you that your life is yours
You only have to look into my eyes
You need to trust me

I have seen where you have been
I have been there before
There is a way out
Take my hand to stop yourself falling
Falling any deeper into darkness

I want you to see the light
To see the future you have ahead of you
The future is yours to choose
The pathway is open to you
Take the step, it isn't that lonely

I will walk with you some of the way
Take my hand
There will be others to take your hand along the way
Until you can stand on your own
You will won't be alone

See my face
Touch my fingertips
Take my hand
And walk with me
Along the pathway to a new future

Tuesday, 30th April 2013 -- The Elephant in the Room

This is the one way that we can avoid someone else feeling so alone in their life:-

The Elephant in the room
Stop talking about me behind my back
Stop looking at me as if I am strange
Talk to me about me
What is it that is so strange

Do I look different to anyone else
Can you actually see inside my head
Can you hear what I am thinking
Are you able to feel what I feel
Why can't you talk about it

Why do you avoid the subject
Are you scared of what I am going to do
What I am going to say
Do you not know what this means to me
I just want to be normal

Why does this have to be avoided
What is it about people that when I mention it
They want to turn and walk away
Why can't you understand
I just need to talk

Why is it that when you avoid the conversation
You just make me feel worse than I already am
Like there is an elephant in the room
You know about it
But, now you don't want to talk about it

I can't keep going like this
It is tiring, perhaps if I just keep myself to myself
Because that way I don't have to worry
Worry about what others or you are thinking
Always thinking I am going to flip or do something strange

If only you had spoken to me
If only you hadn't avoided my conversation
If only you had treated me like a normal human being
I would still be able to carry on
I wouldn't be feeling so alone

Wednesday, 1st May 2013 - Walk with nature

I got up with the dawn chorus with the rising sun, I sat out in the garden this evening listening to the birds sing their evening song as well and it reminded me of how our thoughts are so much like nature in every way :-

Take a walk down the lane
Watch the hedgerow grow
Look at the leaves opening
See the Flowers blowing in the wind
Hear the birds in the sky

Feel the wind through your hair
The sunshining on your face
A warmth on your skin
Melt the cobwebs from your mind
Let the cloud blow away

As you put your hands in your pocket
You put one foot in front of the other
Looking around at what is around you
The brightness after the dark
This maybe the first step, not the last

You can feel a calmness inside
With the beauty around you
Watching the hills roving in front of you
The green fields rolling beside the road
The road straighten a little

As you touch the stone wall
It guides you down the road that lies ahead
Following it at each step
You will soon be joined by others
Others who will touch you

Those others will walk with you
As the road gets wider
The sun gets brighter
More flowers will bring more colour
You will become stronger

As you become stronger
Crossroads will come to you
To join others like you
Others who need a hand
Those who need an ear

Remember the day that you stepped out on the road
The day that others helped you
When you find someone who needs to walk
Who needs to talk
Who needs a guiding arm along the road you have walked

Thursday, 2nd May 2013 - Thinking

I have been sat in the garden enjoying the garden, listening once more to the birds, seeing the bees fly around it helps, I know it won't work completely, to be able to think about the day and blow it away may help to blow some other cobwebs:-

Sit in the garden
Look out on the world
Let the birds sing their hearts out
Whilst you sit and think
Thinking about what has gone

Thinking about who has gone
What has happened between you
Wondering if things could ever settle
Settle to what seems like a normal life
Which everyone else has

Make time to see
What is or who is going to help
Are they sat next to you
Or are they near enough to talk
Look out from under the covers feel the sunshine

Take a peek
You never know who or what is out there
Around the corner
The next phone call, the next text message
The next email

The sun has been shining
So that you can just give one smile
Look out of the window
If you can't go to the garden
See the birds flying the way you would like to

Friday, 3rd May 2013 - Trust

This is truly how I felt today, scared and wondering how I would feel walking in a wood, knowing that this is where I have been for a long time, but, it made me realise that I have someone to help me all the way and that I am not on my own, someone I trust, someone I love and who loves me:-

I took a walk into the woods
They were beautiful and airy woods
With the sun shining through the trees
The twigs under my feet
And a carpet of soon to be glowing Bluebells

I was wondering where I had been before
Somewhere dark
Where the trees climbed above me
I could hear silence
With the birds interrupting every so often

The last time I was there I was on my own
I walked in very slowly
Stood at the edge waiting
Waiting to see if there was someone
This time I walked in with my hand held

My other hand was full with a lead and a camera
I was going in with my eyes wide open
Hoping that at the other end of the carpet of bluebells
There would still be light
I still have a hand holding mine and a shoulder to support me

As the trees got thicker
When the sun went in my head had to keep thinking
Thinking that someone was still walking with me
Someone who wanted to walk with me
Who was willing to walk into the darkest parts

When we got to those darkest parts they held my hand
Pulled me into the light of the wood
Kept me walking the right way
So I could take photos of the right memories
Not remembering the wrong ones

The woodpecker pecking at the tree
As we both walked and talked together
Out of the wood we got into the sun
The photographs of the sunshine on the bluebells
The bluebells which in a week or two will all be blue

As we got to the other side of the wood
The sun was still shining
People walking into my wood
My dream, was no longer my dream
I had been walking through the wood, where I had been before

This time was different
I had a hand to hold, A hand I could trust
I had an ear to listen, An ear to hear me
Instead of being left in the centre of darkness
There was light through the trees with a rock by my side

Friday, 3rd May 2013 - Open Your Eyes to Your Future

I have seen the light finally, it has taken me a long time and a lot of encouragement:-

I have opened my eyes
It is now time for me to smell the roses
To realise that the past doesn't belong
In my future

I want my future to be my time ahead
I want to see what is in front of me
Not just dream it
See the winding path

The path that belongs to me
I want to realise
That all the painful memories
All the hurtful times are gone

The people who have hurt me
It doesn't matter if they are friends, families or foe
They will have no place in my time
My future time, the time that is starting

My future is has new people
It has some of my old people in to support
Most of all new people with new times
That doesn't mean I don't thank those in my past

Whatever has happened
Has helped me straighten up, strengthen up
Repair the broken glass inside me
To become the person with the new future

All I say is I will never forget
Forget means I can't help someone else
It means that I have forgotten what I have grown from
I will have forgotten where I came from to where I am now

What I haven't forgotten
Has helped me support a friend through what I went through
Now they are able to help me and support me
Together we will be stronger person

It may be easier to forget this time
Don't!!
You maybe able to help, talk to or support someone
Open your eyes and see your future

Friday, 3rd May 2013 - Thank You So Much

This is a very soppy poem, so I do apologise, but, it has to be said :-

Thank you
To the one person
Who keeps encouraging me to write
The one person who has had faith in me

There are several others
He is my inspiration
He was the start of them all
And I haven't stopped since

He is my rock, angel and my strength
without him I would not be able to carry on
Without him I wouldn't be sat here
Without him I would be nowhere

He is the one who walks with me
He talks to me
He comforts me
Most of all he wipes my tears and takes my anger

He makes me laugh
He helps me smile
He holds me
He kisses me

Most of all he is there for me
He doesn't care what I am like
As long as I am me
One day I will come back out

He does so much for me
He is the one who is holding my hand through the wood
He is the shoulder I turn to when I am scared
He is the one who has helped me open my eyes to my future

Thank you for loving me
Thank you for holding my hand where you have been before
Thank you for being my light, eyes and rock
I love you very much now and in my new future

Saturday, 4th May 2013 - Blow The Cobwebs Away

What a weird feeling today, the lows of having a high the day before, the thoughts of the past running through my head :-

I have sat awake this morning
Listening to the rain falling
Watching the sun come out
And hearing the wind blowing outside
Whilst my thoughts run away with me

My mind has been thinking about the past
Where it shouldn't be
It has been unhappy
Wanting to get out
It feels like it has now put my future behind bars

The bars are becoming walls
That have been built up around me
Wanting to cause me unhappiness
As it has done before
I hate all this why can just one thought...

One thought turn to many horrible one
Ones that make me want to burst
Today I should be happy
This is the start of a new future
After having such a good day yesterday

I know it doesn't work like that
My lows and highs change like swings and roundabouts
That is the part I can't cope with as well
I know that the bars will come down later
The brick walls will free me as they fall down

There are many ways to help the falling of the walls
To start with is to have a positive thought
To do something for yourself
Even to step outside into the sun
Sit in a park with a book, look around the garden, go for a walk

Take that first step
I am about to go out into the garden
To start to plant my herb garden
This is the first step today
A positive start and thought to help clear the cobwebs

Try the walk
Walk with a friend or among other people
Try to talk to a friend or some other stranger
Most of all try to sit and think with the wind
To help blow the negative thoughts away.

Sunday, 5th May 2013 - A Step Back

I have taken a large step forward, now I have taken some steps back to steady myself to realise that I have taken too bigger step, it doesn't necessarily mean I was wrong, just need to rebalance and take another look at what I did:-

Taking a big step
Take a few more back
It feels good
You just wish you hadn't

Taking a bigger step than you can take
Can help you
Also it can set you back
Baby steps

Walk before striding
Don't take what you think is the biggest leap
Unless you know it is safe
You are safe on the other side

Have someone to catch you
Someone to help catch you with the wobble
The wobble that makes you take steps back
The ones you really don't want to take

Don't be afraid
Take them
The steps back are sometimes needed
To take another few forward

You need to remember
You move forward with strength
It isn't a weakness to realise you have gone back
It isn't bad, you need to do it from time to time

When you take the steps back it is to rest
Rest from taking too many steps forward
As it is a strength to realise you need help
So it is a strength to take those steps back

Never think of yourself as a failure
Because you know that you need help
It is a strength waking up and realising what you want
Weakness is for those around you who say they don't need help

For all those who say that none of this exists
For those who just say snap out of it
When really they don't know
They are the ones who will go through life not understanding

Understanding, this is the first step to what each of us are going through
Time is the next step, it doesn't matter how long
Talking to someone,
Positive thinking, even just one thought for the day, write it down and keep looking at it

Take small steps
Don't be scared of the steps backwards
They help you to rebalance
Write a positive thought down and keep looking at it when you are negative

Sunday, 5th May 2013 - Let Me

I want to help you see the brightness of your future, you have one, you know you do, just let me give you a little encouragement:-

Come out from whatever dark place you are in
Be it a corner, under the duvet, a dark cloud
See the light that shines above you
There is one if you just look
This wondrous light that is not the end

The end of your pain which is your beginning
You are no longer dulling the pain
You are coming head to head with it
You will see the light
The light that is just the beginning

If you come out from your dark place
I respect you
I will take your hand
I will hold it for you very gently
I will not pull you out

You will see the light, the one that is the beginning
The beginning of the end of your pain
The end of your past and the beginning of your new
Where you will take your pain from inside
You will destroy it and start a new life, new future

You finally see the light to your future
Take my hand
We will help each other along the way
We will smile, talk and laugh as we walk
We will take the future together

The light that is shining above you
It is the start to a new day
A new way
A new life and future
Let me help you stand tall and strong against the pain

Sunday, 5th My 2013 - I Will Belong

I have seen the sunshine
I have seen the rain
I have felt the wind blowing
I have touched the grey cloud
I have walked up in the air

The sunshine is outside of my head
It is nowhere inside
I can feel it's warmth on me
But, I still look for it within me
It will shine inside my head to take away the past

I want to be able to get rid of the rain
The rain pouring in my heart
Every time I touch the pain
Of some unforgiving part
One day I will feel it stop, when the pain has dulled

I will belong one day without being pushed out for being what I am "depressed or low" I will be where I want to be:-

I have felt the wind blowing across my face
Once before, even if it was to cool the sun
It feels like there is a pane of glass between me and it
Sometime when it is broken, without the pain
I will feel the wind cooling my skin

I have touched the grey cloud hovering
Hovering over my thoughts and hurt
It won't push past to let in the bright white ones that bring the sun
It will break, when it isn't so long
The grey will go so I can touch the white fluffy one

I have walked up in the air for far too long
I want to walk among the people where I belong
I can watch them going by day by day
Most of all
I want to come back down to earth to walk where I belong

If this is no truth to you
This is just how I feel
I love the sun, the white fluffy clouds and bright blue sky
With this I promise and also hope
I want to belong somewhere one day, without being pushed up and out.

Monday, 6th May 2013 - One Step in the Beautiful Day

When a beautiful day comes along don't hesitate to take it with both hands and try to use it to the best means possible :-

One step forward
But, I know that there will be a step
A step to take backwards
I am going to wait for that

Working in the garden
Walking in the sunshine
Lying on the grass
Letting the dog run around you

What a day it has been today
Not say in my dark corner
Sat on the bed just thinking about the past
Instead I have been looking at my future

You think the sun will have got to my head
Perhaps it has
It has helped me see some things day
Some clearer than others

I have been planting new bulbs
Brushing away the cuttings
Putting out the laundry
Taking photos with new memories

Try the walk into the sunshine!

Tuesday, 7th May 2013 - Lighten the load

Let the thoughts you have help you to unravel and talk to someone:-

Don't give up
Don't let the heaviness weigh you down
Share it
Lighten the load
Talk about it with someone

Don't surrender
To the pain inside
The hurt that has gone on for many years
Talk with someone
Unlock what is making you give up

Life wants to give you a chance
Or you wouldn't be reading this
I want to open your eyes to the chance
It may not be easy
I know it isn't

Whatever has happened will never be erased
Not completely
Whoever has caused it won't be forgotten
Whether they are family, friends or others
It won't be easy

Take a look around the corner
See what your fears are
Find a straight road to walk down
Someone to talk to
Never forget where you have been, you never know when you can help someone else

Wednesday, 8th May 2013 - Shape Your Life

Believe me you don't know how much of this is true especially when someone has been trying to shape it for you, when someone has controlled you, played mind games and done things that would be unbelievable to others and things you think are normal. You are the only one who can shape your destiny, don't let anyone else, it is taking me a very long time to learn this:-

Take your life with your hands
Shape it anyway you want to
Let the sun burn brightly
And lead you where you want to go

Let the rain clear the path for you
The path that will be long and winding
Where it will guide you
To the place where YOU want it to go

Only you can make the choice
Only you can shape your future
Only you can make the change
Only you can ask for help

Take it step by step as the wind guides you
Let it ease you in the right direction
As you step slowly along that path
The path that is lit by the sun

As the day becomes night
So the moon will take over from the sun
With the gentle twinkle of the stars to map your direction
The breeze will still guide you

As you hear the whispering of someone beside you
Remember that is your friend
Helping you with the pain
Holding your hand to support you on the way

You will never know how much it means
To have that hand to hold you
To help you along the way
Along the path of your choice and nobody else's

Thursday, 9th May 2013 - I Want You to Understand

I want to be heard by people, for them to understand what I am going through not just what is on the surface and what they think they know, which for a lot of them is nothing especially about me :-

I am a person
You need to understand
It doesn't matter what is wrong with me
I just need you to understand

I want you to talk to me
To listen to what I have to say
To hear the things I am saying
Without judgement

I am a person
With my own rights
It doesn't matter what is wrong with me
or where

I want you to speak to me
Without any convictions or reasoning
I want you to listen
To what I need to say

I am a person
Who stands up tall, sits down in a corner
It doesn't matter how
I am still a normal human being not an animal

I want you to see me
For who I am
Not just for what is inside my head
I want you to see past the surface

I AM a person
I count
I want to be heard
I will shout it to you so you can hear me

I just want you to understand

Friday, 10th May 2013 - Left Out

This is my feelings today all day, I have been pushed away as though I am stupid or an idiot or there is something wrong:-

Feeling left out
As though the whole world has left you behind
I do too
Feeling like you are in a corner where you belong

Everyone says that they want you
Yet they still leave you alone
Someone tells you are needed
But you are still feeling left out in the cold

Think about tomorrow
Get yourself amongst the crowd
Talk to someone
Nudge them and say I do exist

I am here
I have every right for you to treat me as part of it
Hear what I have to say
You can't push me away

I want to be heard
I want to join in
I want to be part of it
Why won't you let me

Saturday, 11th May 2013 - Help Me Understand!

Help Me to understand what I am going through, have you ever sat and thought about it or ever asked someone what they can see in you especially when you are feeling low or unhappy:-

I want to understand
Understand what you are telling me
You are telling me you are normal
And I am normal

How can I be normal
My mind isn't well, I'm not well
You are telling me that it will get easier
That I can get help

That you are helping me
By making me realising that something is wrong
That I am normal even though I am ill
You are talking to me why then?

You tell me you want to support me
Why is it I don't want to be around people
I thought this feeling was wrong
I want to feel normal not just for you to tell me

Help me seem like things are right
I want to feel happy all the time not just half
I want to reach the sky again
I want to feel the solid ground under my feet

Why do people not want to bother
Why do they think I am going to break as soon as they touch me
Or even talk to me
I don't understand why my moods are swinging

I have walked and talked
To myself and I can't get the answers
Which is why I am asking you as you say this is normal
Tell me how can this be normal?

I want to understand
I want others to understand
Who I am behind the sadness and pain
Not just what they see at face value and take it as just a bad mood!

Help me understand
You say this is normal
Tell me what normal is
Tell me what I am going through.

Help Me!!!

Saturday, 11th May 2013 - Help me I'm scared

I need help to stop me from being scared of doing my normal everyday life things:-

Scared of being with people
People who you know
That is how I am feeling
People who aren't sure about how to talk to me

Have you ever cried
Because you are unsure about seeing people
I am at this point
I will get over this, but, I can't today

I can't sit here and accept I am going to be here all day
I have to move and get myself something to eat and drink
I can't be so rude and not let someone in
Just because I am scared

I am sat in a dark corner
Not wanting to come out
I want to feel safe when I am walking around
But, I'm not, I'm scared, I feel my pain

I feel the tears rolling down my face
As the pain of being alone is scaring me
It is hurting so much as if I am not going to get out of this
I am working on a normal life

I'm not sure how much longer I can cope
How much longer I can cope living like this
Expecting someone to be there all the time for me
Wanting someone to support me or knowing if they will support me

This is why I want someone to help me to understand

Help me I'm scared perhaps of understanding!!

Sunday, 12th May 2013 - Control

Ever felt that you had control of everything and then suddenly it losing it? :-

How can I be so scared of losing a grip
Losing a grip of control on my life
When I haven't ever really had that grip
All my life, there has been someone controlling me

When I think I have control
Someone has just come whizzing by
Taken control of life
It has slipped through my fingers

I am trying ever so hard
To keep holding tight
It feels like it is all slipping away from me
I am sitting doing the only thing I can control writing

My thoughts have runaway with me
Losing control
It is the scariest part of what is happening
Not knowing how to take the control back

Thursday, 16th May 2013 - How do I explain?

I am sorry to have been away a few days, but, I have been taken down with a sick bug. I wrote this to try to explain how I am feeling and have been with a friend who can't understand:-

How do you explain
That you can't talk to someone
You can't hear them
You want to but you can't

How do you explain
How you are feeling right now
That you want to be like them
But you can't

How do you explain
Why you can only write down
Write what you are feeling
Because you can't talk

How do you explain
What is in your head
Why you are feeling like you are
You can't

How do I explain to you
I still love you as a friend
But I don't know how to be a friend
I can't, you have to trust me

You have to understand
I can't talk
I can't feel
I can't explain

Trust me one day I will
Trust me, and stay by me
Take my hand and talk to me
There is no other explanation

Thursday, 16th May 2013 - Life is Like Music

I am not sure why I have used music before, but here goes and see what you think, see if you which sheet you are:-

Life is like music
Full of highs and lows
For a lot of us the music goes
An octave lower for a longer period than others
Whilst there are very short periods of high

For some of us we dance
Dance a sad dance to that music
We may mooch
We may just sit and listen
Whilst it plays our sad song

As the music plays on with bars
As rules
The rules we hate, but keep us on the steady
It stops us from wondering
Every so often we stray from the stave even beyond the bars

The notes that are playing
We aren't even hearing, because we can't
There is too much noise in your head
The bars aren't making sense and neither is the stave
The words are all blurred looking like the black hole as they move together

Everyone is different in many different ways
Some will always stay with the sheet of music in front of them
Some will chop and change as will the key
Some will lose the sheet altogether
Others will find and lose this sheet of music along the way

If you have worked out which shee you are
You know where you life is
The music will keep on playing no matter what
It is just up to you to make the changes if you want
Or stay the same, you only have one tune it will keep on playing until you change it

I know that I keep losing and finding
This will be the last time my music will be a blur
I will keep playing out loud for those around me
I want to be able to find my music
I want to play it with those standing by me

Friday, 17th May 2013 - Being Scared

It's alright for everyone to say 'I don't understand why you are like this, I have gone through so much and I'm not like you' If you only knew how I felt, if only I could understand why I can't be like you as well, I only wish I could walk into the open and say yes, I am a beautiful and amazing woman, but I can't this poem will help you to understand what I can say to you:-

Being scared
Of what happens next
What you need to do
The next step
What changes are needed

Being scared
Of people around you
People who love you
People who want to help you
Knowing who is going to stand by you

Being scared
Of taking control of things
Not knowing if they are the right things
Wanting to make the difference
What is positive and what isn't

Being scared
Of the whole World around you
Because of the constant pushing and shoving
What could next hit you in the face
Why people look at you strangely

Being scared
Of being the elephant in the room
That nobody knows how to talk to
Nobody wants to break you
Wanting to be treated and talked to normally

Being scared
Of constantly being in the corner or behind a brick wall
The places you want to get out of
But you don't know how
You want to see the room and World

I have been all of these things above
My heart has cried a thousand tears
I have shouted a million times
Nobody heard me
Until now I have someone who helps me

I won't say I don't feel scared
Because I do and of all the above
I am just scared of not understanding
Why I am this way, why I am scared and crying
I know there will be a day

I know there will be a way out of all of this

Saturday, 18th May 2013 - Don't Let the Clock Pass too Much

I have had time to think whilst I have been sick this week about how I am letting time passing me by on things of the past when I really have a bright enough future ahead of me, that doesn't mean I am cured or I am going to stop feeling low, it means I want to start to dig myself out of my hole, from out of my corner or under the duvet if you want:-

Second by second
Minute by Minute
Hour by hour
Day by day
Month by month

Everything changes
by each fraction of time we take
Each heart beat that is made
Every step is fresh
To a place where we haven't been

The place may be new
It may be old
But with each passing second
Something changes
No matter how we feel

The time that ticks by
Is time that spaces the old from the new
We need to stop and think
About how we can change our thoughts
From the past to the future

With each passing tick
Tock is passing by
We are being left behind in the past
Needing to think about what lies ahead
Inside is the urge to see ahead

We want to see what lies in front
What our lives are always going to turn into
But only we can make it happen
Only we can make the change
We have to take the next step

As each second passes by
Why waste the opportunity
Of finding something new out
Something that might help be rid of the past
Sometimes we have to say goodbye in order to say hello

Take my hand
Step with me
To somewhere we have never been
Somewhere we are destined to go
To the future my friend

How much longer can we wait
How much more should make our past
A sad and bad past that we need to throw away
We need to hold onto the light that is in front
An step into it

Please hear me when I say
That as the clock ticks by
Let the past tock away
Take my hand into the future
With each new step into the light

Each month gone by
Each week going past
Each day we forget
Each hour we throw away
Each minute we will see what happens

Don't let the clock pass too much

Saturday, 18th May 2013 - Loneliness

I will warn you that this might be painful to read, but, it is just how I have felt even though I have someone to support me and talk to it is just how I have felt, if it hadn't been for that person I would have done exactly what I have said in this poem:-

Loneliness is such a solitude thing
It is so isolated
It is so painful
And harmful to the soul

Loneliness can cause so much damage
Hurt
And unwillingness to live
It can cause so much injury to oneself

Loneliness can do so much to one
It is not good for anyone
There is a difference between
Being on your own and being alone

Some of us have been lonely for far too long
That is where it is scary to start to step out
Stepping out of being lonely
It hurts, but that first step will lead to many

Make sure you have someone with you
To step out with you
To stop the loneliness the thing that hurts the most
This will be the next step

One small step at a time
It won't stop it completely
It will just help to stop it
This will then help you to learn the difference

Being on your own
Is the space you have around you
Being alone is the pain that surrounds you
Speak to someone to help stop that pain

Loneliness can surround you even in a crowd
I know how it feels
I have been there, people talking, you feel alone
Nobody wants to talk about you or to you

Loneliness is hurtful
It is painful
You can stop it by talking to someone
By making that first move

I'm going to, today

Saturday, 18th May 2013 - Being a Third Person

I went through this only today and this is how it has made me feel, so much so that I wish I had stayed at home:-

It is sad to feel like a third person
In everything that is done
I am the last person
I am the one that is third in line

I want to feel like I have a voice
But I don't
I want to feel like someone puts me first
It is never going to happen

I am the last one in
So I am the last one out
Being the last person
Means everyone is watching me

Watching every move I make
When they don't realise what is inside
Or don't understand
I can't be talked to even though I am crying inside

I know that I am not meant to feel like this
But I do
I want to talk, it doesn't matter
I need to talk it really doesn't matter

I am just a small part of someone else's life
I am the one that has interrupted their routine
I have upset things
It doesn't matter about me, if I cry in a corner

All I am is a third person going through depression, I don't matter

Sunday, 19th May 2013 - One Small Step for Me

Today is my first day of socialising with a few people I know with my rock by my side, it is to help a friend when they need it so if you want to call it killing two birds with one stone you can or even taking two steps and it is a little too much don't this is my choice and my chance to help someone else other than myself:-

Today is a brave new day
A day in which I am trying to put a smile on
Not paint one on
I meet with an old friend on their special day
It's not a day for me to spoil

Today I will probably talk
Talk about what has happened to me
What is going on inside my head
Something I find difficult
As I don't understand what is going on

Today will be scary
As I may have to relive my past
In order to get to my future
Something I want to hide away
The scary parts I keep locked away

Today may be of untold parts
Pain and hurt
As old as the friend is
They don't know all of my past
Especially what is hidden behind a closed heart

I no longer want to hide
I want to look forwards to my future
With this future it claims my past
Not totally forgetting it
Just allowing it to be easier to cope

For me not to get into low moods
For me to no longer take tablets
For my friends to have me back to my normal self
I have to take this step
Nobody said it was easy going back to me again

I want to be amazing
I want to be strong
I want to be the bubbly, vivacious me again
I know it is going to be painful
But I also know I need people to help me

What will happen today
Is a new step
A small step into a new part of my life
When it is all done
It will be one I can look back on as my choice and my chance to change

Monday, 20th May 2013 - For Every Small Step Taken

I believe that I have taken some very small steps this weekend towards making the small changes in my life which may go towards the larger future of my life:-

For every small step that is taken
One small change to your life is made
One small word that is spoken
By friends or family
Means there may be some understanding

Even if that small understanding is yours
That your friends are there for you
So you can help them understand what you are going through
So they know that beneath the painted smile is pain
They know that for all the years you haven't known them you have history too

It hurts to think that just because you have a good day
That is how you are all the time
That you are better and there is nothing more wrong
How sad that is
How painful it is someone can think that you can just snap out of it

Because there are people who can just snap out of it
There are times it is easier said than done
There will be times when a smile glows
But behind the smile is the broken glass
The tears flowing from your heart

I don't want to just paint a smile
I want the smile to be real
I want every day to be a good day
Not just yesterday because I was with friends
Because I want to be happy all the time

Happiness starts with you though
It starts with that small change
The change that is acceptable to your life
One that will make that difference
One that will give you the sunshine back

I know that it will happen
And with a thought like that in mind
There is nothing better to think about
It is the most positive thought I can give right now
I also know it is quite powerful too

My past will ease into my future
The glass will be crushed into the path I walk on
It won't ever go away it will just get easier
See the light that guides you
To the bright future ahead

Tuesday, 21st May 2013 - Imagine

Very short and sweet, with nothing to help except, close your eyes and sit back imagine the image of this poem

The wood pigeon cooing from the fields
The songbirds are singing from the trees
The sun is still shining over the country side
Over the bright yellow fields of Rapeseed

The quietness around them
So I can think to myself
About the day I have had
Time for me time

A glass of wine in one hand
The sound of my laptop humming
As I sit back and think of the wondrous creatures outside
Soon I will hear the sound of a Tawny as the night draws near

The warmth of the evening
Flowing through my windows
With a slight breeze coming through to cool
I sit back and think what a lovely evening it is

Wednesday, 22nd May 2013 - Turn it Around

I think I am finally understanding what I am being told, I am starting to get a voice to control my life, to turn the pain into my new future :-

How to explain how I feel
I'm not sure
I am quiet
I'm not upset
I'm not ecstatic either

Perhaps calm
Calm before the storm
Which I'm not looking for
I am looking for peace
Perhaps it is that, peace

Peace within myself
Maybe I have finally found this
Within me
Walking instead of running
Thinking to help me understand

To understand
For me to be able to help myself
With the pain that has been hurting for too long
The pain that can be laid to rest
By numbing, it will never go away

I will just be able to deal with it
To take the edge off it
So I can think how I can turn it
Turn it to the positive in my future
Not to be just the negative of my past

I want to use it to my advantage
Instead of it taking advantage of me
I am going to manage it
Not it managing me
I am the only manager of my life

No-one will ever control me again
Not even the pain inside
I am finally taking my life in both hands
It will take a while
But, I will do it step by step

All through the positive pain of the past
Finally I am starting to understand
What I have gone through
I can take control of
You can do the same

Thursday, 23rd May 2013 - You are My Rock

I have only a few friends in this world and they are the ones that count, the ones I can number on one hand. These are the people who have helped me through a horrible and painful past, letting go of my hand lightly to lead me onto a new and beautiful future to a new person who will help me get past the pain of the past to help me deal with it. My advice is, find someone who can help you read my poem and hopefully you will cry as I have to write it:-

You have held me since the first day
The first day I met you
You held my look
As I held yours through the warm sunshine
What I didn't know was what was going to happen next

I know that you will always hold me
You have held me so lightly at times
I can hardly feel it
And I have thought you were letting go
Now I realise that you have always been there

I can see you everywhere I go
There is something to tell me that you
You won't let me go
You are then whenever it is dark
So that you can guide me through

If it wasn't for the darkness which I have been in
I would never have realised what you have done for me
I maybe thinking about the past
But it is the past that has brought me to you
The past that will be left behind one day

As you steady me with your strong hand and shoulder
I am able to stand up and walk
I am able to sit here and think clear enough
I have moved on through my work
I will be able to get on and have a more positive future

As you put your arms around me
I can hear you say my name
Which is when I realise that I have someone
Someone who loves me, cares about me and understands me
Understands me without having to be false

I have felt the love from your heart
And I feel more and more each day as I do for you
What you have done for me is beyond words
You are my best friend, rock, lover, a shoulder and the one person who understands
Understands what I am feeling inside

I know you will say that
I am the one that has made the change
I am the one that has done the things needed
But you are the one that has been there for me
This is why I held on for so long so you could be strong

You are a strong person
I have held you in my arms
I can talk to you
I am at peace when I am with you
I may cry inside and out, but I can't with anyone else

You listened to me
When others could not hear
You saw the pain
When others just walked past it
You are the one person I have trusted with what I know

I love you and always will.
More than yesterday, more tomorrow.
You are my rock and my light
You are always there and holding my hand
Thank you hun and thank you to my best girlfriend too
I wouldn't and couldn't do this without either of you

Thursday, 23rd May 2013 - Talk to Me!!

Lift the wall, the wall that has been between you and I for a long time, one you won't lift because you won't talk about it:-

What I want to know is..
Why do you look past me
Why can you not see what my friends see
If you can see it, why can't you talk about it
Let me help you understand what they see

I want to talk about me
I want to help my pain
Help it to ease into the background
I don't want to forget it
As it has helped me move to my future

I just to be able to talk about it
Without it hurting
I know that if someone just talked
The elephant would go away
If people weren't so judgemental it would be easier

Take the time to talk to someone
Someone who is sat alone
Someone who looks like they need to talk
Someone who wants to talk
Talk about my mental health

I want to tell you how I am feeling
Instead of saying I'm fine
When really I am very low
And that I am painting this false smile for you
For everyone around me

If you didn't find my mental health a problem
I would be taking to you now
But you just judge me or tell me to snap out of it
If I could talk to you it would help me
And it would help others

Talk to me!! I only have depression

Thursday, 23rd May 2013 - My Loneliness

I wanted you to see how my evening has progressed to loneliness:-

Feeling Lonely and being alone
Two different things
Never think they are the same
Tonight I am lonely
I want to be with someone, but, I can't.

Lonely is being on your own
But you don't want to be
This draws you down a dark road
One that grows as the silence does
Loneliness hurts

Sitting alone
Can lead to loneliness
But, don't let it
There are times when you don't want others
You want to be a lone

Loneliness is painful
I have had so much of that over the years
I don't know how to cope
Cope with being around so many people
Having busy weekends and evening

Even though I have been with someone
I have been lonely
I have never felt with them
There has been a loneliness that echoes inside
Until now, I have now found someone I am with

I am only lonely
When I am not with them and that is on nights like this
When I am sat on my own
Listening to music and crying
It is a time when my positive thoughts get pushed aside

The tears in my heart fall
Then they fall from my eyes
It feels like someone has ripped something from me
The summer evening is going
So am I, I wish I could get my positive thoughts back

Friday, 24th May 2013 - Talk

Talk to someone, you don't know how helpful it may be, text, write, talk, it helps to me talking to you through my poetry helps and to be able to write down how I feels makes things a little easier, I do talk to my partner as well, but, I suppose I write down more than I can say, he still reads it all there is nothing to hide, I just find this way easier, try it and write it in a comment on my blog, share them with others as I do, lift this World's ideas of Mental Health and show that we can think as well as being ill!!
:-

I sat driving today in the pouring rain
With the wind blowing down
And the sun shining the other way
When I was listening to the radio
I heard my favourite song

I smiled to myself
Which helped me for the half day I was doing
The breakfast I was about to eat
The cappuccino I was about to drink
And the text I was going to write

The text read this way
Morning, beautiful I am now at work
I am alright, when I realised I wasn't
I was trying to tell my man
That things were good when they weren't

Even with the song I listened to
The drive into work and seeing the sun
Nothing was going to change
I then went home after taking my heart off my sleeve
I did my shopping and pulled up outside

I got out of the car
Taking in all my bags I got through the door
Finally closing the door to the elements
And the world outside
I now had to deal with my World inside

This couldn't be held back now I was at home
I put down my bags and unpacked them
I got changed from my work clothes and shoved them in to wash
As I stood by the machine I burst into tears
I could no longer hold back

My day hadn't been a bad one
In fact it was good
The only problem was my heart was heavy
So heavy I couldn't hold it in any longer
My rock and love looked at me wondering why I was crying

I explained that I didn't know except
I had been at work with a painted smile
Even though I felt heavy in heart
I had just wanted to cry
There was no way of doing it except at home

With this he put his arms around me
Asking if there was anything I needed to talk about
About why I was feeling like this
I just said no that him holding me was enough
So that's what he did

My heart started to feel lighter
As he stood with his arms around me
Knowing that I was finally home in my baby's arms
I also knew that I was having time to think
Think about positive things

The moral to this poem is it doesn't matter who you are
Who you choose
Talk to someone
It does ease the hurt and the heart

It may not take it away, but, talk it doesn't matter who it is

Friday, 24th May 2013 - It Helps to Talk

It helps you to talk, it has helped me listen to my story:-

An evening of doing things with someone
Someone who supports me
Doing things that we should do
He doesn't just support me through talking to me
He supports me through life

He helps me to sort me out
Helps me with my shopping
Doing the boring things
Doing the enjoyable things
Even the things that really have to be done

When I met him
I found him stood in a kitchen surrounded by things
He had just moved
Now ten months on my life wouldn't be worth living
He has done so much for me

I will also say I have helped him too
I never forgot the times when I have been depressed
I never walked away
I stood by him and I still do now
Until it was time for me to finally shut down

I sat at the edge of the bed
I cried
But, I knew that he was ready
He was strong enough
He shouted at me once, but, only because he didn't know how

He has never stood by
To watch someone fall apart
He has never seen some just cry and cry and cry
Crying for something he couldn't help with
Cry for something they didn't understand

Now we both talk to each other
Just as a couple do
We both stand together
Just like any couple do
Most of all we are building strength and our lives together

Not everyone will be as lucky or fortunate as I have been
But you do have someone to talk to
It may not be someone like I have
But if you have anyone
Talk to them

Help them to understand what you are going through

Saturday, 25th May 2013 - I Am an Individual

I have sat here for a long time and let others control me for so long and now it is time for me to change and my choice it is only ME that can do this:

I am an individual
I stand out from the crowd
Because I sit in the dark corner over there
I have been in the crowd for far too long
Not realising that I am me

I am me
I have problems of my own
I am no different
I have just had to drop out of it for a while
So I can get myself back on track

I am that person
I am still the person you have seen before
I just need time and to talk
To talk to someone
Who will give me that time

It doesn't matter
If you don't want to understand
Because I will just let you go
I know that you are judging me by what is going on in my head
I don't need judgement, I need understanding

I have to let go of the past
I have to get go of the people who have hurt me
To let go of the people who have caused pain
If you are one, I am sorry
I have to do it

I need people to understand
I will explain it to help you
But, if you judge me it will hurt
That is the time I will let go
My past is too painful for me not to voice

I have had enough control in my life
It is my time to choose
I will do as I want to
I will choose who I want to be
But it is me who has to change it

If I don't make the change
Nobody will
If they do, it means I am back to square one
I have been there for too long
I will help you understand if you want to

Saturday, 25th May 2013 - Trust

Trust is a massive thing, to trust someone to talk to I have learnt that throughout the animal kingdom we are all the same Listen to what I have to say:-

I basked in the beautiful sunshine
With beautiful creatures
This helped my thoughts flow
To what I wanted to say

I wanted to fly with these creatures
Saw through the sky
If only my dreams could go that high
Why oh why couldn't I

When I looked into their eyes
They had sorrow and torment
As had I
They had learnt to imprint to a human

I walked around with them for an hour
Learning about them and their habits
I learnt that I needed to be like them
And trust the one I am with

Trust is the only thing I have
It is an issue of the person ever leaving me
I know he won't
After all that we have done and gone through

I want to be able to talk someone
Someone I feel secure with
Someone I feel safe with

Someone I want to spend the rest of my life with

Sunday, 26th May 2013 - Why Can't You Understand?

I am here talking about something that happened today, not just to me but to anyone who is going through depression, It is something I can't help but argue "Why can't you understand?"

Where do I stand if you
Don't understand
How can I make others understand
That I can be as low as I am now
As I want to explain, but, you aren't listening

I want you to hear
Hear what I have to say
Hear that this isn't my normal self
It is the tablets that are helping me
To feel happy, to be me

How do I explain
That I have to work for money
I spend all my hours in work
Surrounded by people and painting on a smile
Making sure, nobody catches me out

I want to get through this
If you can't understand, it isn't going to happen
I have been controlled in my lifetime enough
Now is my life and even though you don't understand
I need you to understand I am the fat controller of my life

If you don't want to understand
That is fine too
I will keep explaining it, may be you may open your ears
But, I need people in my life who are going to get me
Who are going to understand what I am going through

I will walk through the crowd on my own one day
I will stand tall on the mountain top by myself one day
I will swim the roughest seas one day
I will look into the brightest sun with the biggest smile one day
Remember it is me you have missed, me you could not see

Sunday, 26th May 2013 - I want....

I want to be heard and to change my life:-

As the tears fall from my heart
How do I explain
That I'm not as strong as I was
That even though I am strong enough to accept
I am not strong enough to get through

That I can't help the tears from my eyes
The sorrow in my heart
That I want to change my life
The way it has been in the past
And change it to the future

I want to be able to scream and shout
Not to keep quiet and keep it all in
So that I can have my voice heard
To my choice and not someone elses
To be able to sound my voice in a crowd

I want to be heard
I want to be seen
I want to stop living in the dark
I want the sun to shine down
I want to feel the rain in my hair

All I want is for you to understand me
Understand the tears
Being on my own
Needing to be with you
Wanting someone to support me

Monday, 27th May 2013 - Don't Hide behind the pain

I feel that I needed to tell you this because I am not all smiles or all sorrow, I am doing this to be able to be heard by you and others around me, that I have done wheat you might be doing and that is hiding behind the pain, but I want you to turn that negative to a positive and find someone to turn to:-

Today has been the first day
The first day of this weekend
Where I didn't have to paint my smile on
Or to be strong to go out and enjoy myself

Saturday I was out in the beautiful sunshine
Happy and smiling
Amongst crowds of different people
People who didn't know me

I was also with my support
I know was feeling the same way as me
Many people have commented on a picture
One where I was laughing and smiling

The first they had seen in such a long time
As did they with my partners
We flew the birds that we both adore
Birds in the future when we are both well enough we will keep

We booked this a long time ago
But I still had to work myself up to this day
To help myself get in the right frame of mind
I then went home to family

My partners family who stayed the weekend
It was lovely to see them
But because they were on my ground I was feeling nervous
I wanted to be normal and hide my depression

I couldn't
It came out when something started
I went off in tears, I upset the lovely day
My partner sat and explained everything

They understood
It isn't that I am ashamed
It was because I didn't want them as new family
To feel I was different

I didn't want them to think that I had copied my partner
When they talked to me they said they didn't
The whole upset was nearly forgotten
Everyone is happy again

The reason I am telling you this
Is because it is no good hiding
It will all come out
Your family need to know to help you

I know that mine is a new family
The last thing that was said as they left
Message me if you need to talk
Which means such a lot

Even though I have sat here on my own today
It has been quite pleasant
As I have been surrounded by people all weekend
I needed time on my own

My partner has been with me and his mum
My support at home
What is more I have if I needed to got friends
Friends I can message or talk to and new friends

Through my writing I want to help you
Help you to understand what I am going through
To help you see what a pickle you can get in hiding
Especially from friends and family

I want you to understand that if they turn their backs
You know that they will never understand
That you have others to help you
There are a lot of people to talk to.

Please hold your hand out, open your mouth and ask you will never know
Don't hide behind the pain

It honestly doesn't help you

Monday, 27th May 2013 - I Want Someone To Hear You

I want someone to be able to hear you, but until you ask for help or do something about it nobody will, I have learnt it the hard way over my lifetime and now it has got worse that it has ever been, I am now with someone who wants to help me with friends and family to talk to and I have let it all out, please if not for you do it for the ones you love:-

I want to listen to somebody else
I want to hear about their pain
To be able to turn their life around
I would like to tell them how you turn the pain to the future
I know I can't yet, I can only listen

I would like to stop the stabbing pain in my chest
To hear my heart beating
Not crying or bleeding
The pain I feel to turn it into something positive
So I can fly through the open door freely and stay there

The door that is so wide open
My wings haven't grown strong enough
To fly through
I keep being sucked back to the past
Where I can still feel the pain and sorrow

I know I will never forget the pain and the sorrow
But, I know that it will ease enough
So I can be happy with my new life
In my new life
One that will include a new family and new love

I have found love
However it is getting past the old pain
The pain of what my past did to me
I also know that if it wasn't for my past I wouldn't be here
Where I am sitting talking to you now

I know you are thinking what has this got to with me
You will never forget the pain or how it feels
What will happen is the pain will be less sharp
If you learn to get past it
Or if you want to, if you don't you won't

I have kept my pain locked up for far too long
I let the new love of my life go through his pain first
So that when he was strong enough he could in turn
Help me through mine
The trouble is mine has now just got too painful

It has taken me until now to realise it
You have to let it out or the tears will keep flowing
You have to shout or it will keep locked in
You have to want to change the pain or it will change you

Most of all you need to ask for help because someone will hear you

Monday, 27th May 2013 - My Honesty

You want to know what my pain is, I have written a little about it. I can't go into the full story or you will never believe me, the tears and pain I am trying to take the edge from to help towards my future I have a lot of it, it has taken me a lot of courage to tell you today:-

If you want me to be honest
I am going to be
My life has been full of people controlling me
If there was at any time I was free and I have misinterpreted it
I have been reined back in to be controlled again

I have had things forced on me when I said no
So many times that the smells surrounding them
Have not helped me into new relationships
I am fortunate enough to have a beautiful man standing by my side
Someone who is willing to help and understand

The pain of being unable to have a normal relationship
Is humongous and you may never understand
Because I have security and trust issues as well
Again I have someone standing by my side
Someone who understands

This is painful writing it down
I know that I need to tell you what has happened to me
For me to be under this such up and down dark cloud
I have someone who wants me to be me
To have a pint of beer at a restaurant meal if I want not forced a glass of wine to be a lady

Not to have to dress up in skirts to go out
He wants to me to be me
He wants the bubbly vivacious young lady he met back
My support, my rock, my love
Does not want to control what I say, where or do

I am not held back because the job I am about to apply for is earning more than him
I will not be dictated to who my friends are going to be
Nothing about me embarrasses him
Everything I do he loves and encourages
My life now is my future

I just want to take the edge from the pain
So I can live with it
I want to campaign to bring an understanding of mental health in work places
I want other people to know we are normal
We are people who have problems in our past to get past into our future

I want to be pain free and to talk a little more easier without tears
Tears down my face
Or tears in my heart
Without the need to be holding onto someone else's strength
To be a short, beautiful, amazing woman working her past towards her future

Tuesday, 28th May 2013 - Change? Are you ready?

I have decided to take one more step to help myself change me, to be able to get my life back on track, I am ready for it to talk to someone else, are you?

What a day?
It is never a good day to go back to work on
But you just never know
Keep your head down, keep working it may just get better

A peacefully quiet surroundings
With the open fields around me
There is a beautiful field of yellow to the side
With a field of green to the front
And a ploughed field to the back

The sun is just setting
Shining the bright yellow like a dream
It is settling down behind the brown ploughed field
As I sit here listening to the birds around

There are thoughts running through my head
Thoughts that I am just starting to realise
Realise that may be I am not as bad as I am
That may be I am worth living with

Thoughts that have relaxed me
Have chilled me out since last week
That it is me who has to change
It is me who has got to take the first step

I can't let people change me
Or I am back where I was before
I just want to know how to help my pain
Tomorrow I am going to talk to the right person

I am going to talk to someone
Someone other than my other half to help me
At this moment I know he is smiling at me
I also know that I need someone to help

Someone to help me
Me to turn this pain into something useful
Turn the anger to a smile
Someone who can help me to turn the negative to a positive

I want to be helped, I want to change, I want my life back on track

Do you?

Tuesday, 28th May 2013 - Scars for Change

I have enough scars to help not only me, but, you as well, hear me, listen to what I have to say don't push me aside:-

I will tell you the rest of my honesty
Whilst I have been telling you to change
I have done little by little
One of my first steps was this poetry blog
Whatever you think about it

I have been in the darkest hole for so long
I am not meaning days, months, years
I am meaning decades
I have not been able to dig myself out of it
It isn't until now that I have really understood how long

I have hidden in and out of shadows
I have been my bubbly self
Thinking that everything is alright
I have finally found someone to stand by me
Who knows how I feel or how I have felt

I have found someone to hear me
Someone to hold me
Someone who will sit and dry my tears
Someone who will cry with me
Someone who loves me for the me behind everything

He doesn't look at the sadness
He doesn't find things to hurt me time and time again
He holds me close to stop the pain
Wishing he could take it away all the decades of pain
I wish that I could step out and be me again

That is all I want
I want the pain to go away
But I know that it won't go away wholly
It will take time and will only ease
I also know that I can turn it to my advantage, my positive, my future

I have so many more steps to take
They will be baby ones, but, one by one I will make them
I will slowly walking into the light
I know that I have so many friends to help me
I know I have some family to stand by me

There will be tears
There will be screaming
There will be anger
There will be a lot of anger
Soon enough all that will change to something I want laughter

I will finally become the person
That I want to be and everyone thinks I am
I will not stop the fight for anyone else
I will still be here for those who need me
I will help the fight for the lift of stigmatism on mental health

I will help to change the thoughts for mental health
As I have the scars for it all
But those scars will help me to change my life and yours

Tuesday, 28th May 2013 - I Am Sorry I Don't Speak Just Write

Feeling the aches tonight feel this poem:-

Did you feel the knives stabbing in your heart
The aching in your back
Stones being thrown at your head as the tears fall
The bruises on your body
The bleeding from your legs

I have too
Now that is starting to ease
It will never go
But there have been things that have helped
I have had people encouraging me

Encouragement that has been taken in small steps
I have done one step at a time
Each poem I have written for you so far
Is the pain I have felt
I have just hit the nail on the head

I am not a speaker of any sort
I write, this is why I can tell you more than I can speak
I find it easier in writing
My heart breaks to tell you all
I am not sure you want to hear it

I want to be able to tell you
Tell you to do the same,
Write it down
Listen to some music and just write
You can tell a story or your feelings

Please write with me
I want you to feel how I feel
Sometimes it is liberating
I don't care if people don't like it
The next one they may well doe

It helps me
To become the person I need to be
The person I want to be
To come out of the dark corners I have been dodging
This time will be the last time

This won't be the last time I help
I will keep shouting until it is clear
Very clear that we only have something wrong
We are not persons to be ignored

We will be heard and understood

Wednesday, 29th May 2013 - One more step

One small step for others but one big step for me:-

One step at a time
It doesn't matter how small
I have done so much lately
I'm not sure if it has all been too quick

I make one more step tonight
But this is important
This is the one change in my life that is a must
This is one step that has to be

As I take this step tonight
I want you to think how you can change
How you can make something different
Put your thoughts onto paper

Write a comment below this one
Let me hear what they are
It doesn't matter what it is
Or how small it is

I have been painting a smile for so long
I want to change it to a real one
I am going to meet someone
Someone who could and will change my life

To you it may not be a very big thing
For me at this moment in time it is a step
The step that will help me
Help me to get my life back on track

Wednesday, 29th May 2013 - My Words Will Speak

Start writing, if you are reading this you have a computer or some way of being able to write even a verse, write down how you feel, no-one is going to judge you I certainly am not, I know that mine aren't great, but, the more you read and write the better you will feel and not only that you can add it to the bottom of my pages and post them :-

My voice can't be heard
So I write
I write about what I know
I know and understand
About depression

I know that I have had a lifetime
A lifetime to going in and out of dark corners
Being scared of people
Not being able to stand up to them
I know what it is to hide because it is easier

Easy is what I did back then
Until last year
Last year I took one huge and massive step
To move away from what had made me
What I am now a wreck

I wanted to get out of my life so badly
I wrote books
I wrote poems
They were read
What I didn't know was how much I needed and wanted to write

I'm not like a lot of people
Talking to people is difficult
Speaking in public is not my thing
Telephoning someone when I am out of work
These are not easy, but, give me a keyboard

I want to write about the topic
The topic that has been with me all my life if I am truthful
Just sometimes it was deeper than usual
I have finally come out into the open
I am not just open to my friends, but, to the public, my readers

I enjoy writing my thoughts
Because not only are they mine
Sometimes they are yours too
This was one change I made to help me
Help me to get through my depression

Help me to be honest with myself
With the one person who supports me
I hide behind the pain
When I could use the pain to help me
Turning it to my advantage by helping someone else

I have helped the person who is supporting me
Helped him through his mental break down
Now we support each other, him supporting me more
What I now need to do is turn this pain to positive thoughts
I want to feel good about myself

I know don't we all
But, I want to stop putting myself down
As so many have over the years
I need the confidence boost
And I do this through my writing

Keep on reading
Start writing
You will never know how good it makes you feel

Wednesday, 29th May 2013 - I Want to Love Me

You and I want to love me for me:-

I want to love me for me
I want to lead a normal life
Hold my head up high
Straighten my back
Walk through a crowd with a smile

First of all I need to think
Think about the good things in my life
Start to think about the positive things
The things that are good in my life
To let them over take what has happened in my past

I want to say that my past has helped me
I have realised that I wouldn't be where I am
I know that my future is much brighter
I want to remember that I have a new family
I have new friends

I just have to remember to take one step
One baby step at a time
I smile every day
But I also cry maybe not on the outside
But in my heart, for the years I have lost

Instead of dwelling on the past
I want to think about my future
A bright new future
With a bright new life
Like you I have to take it a step at a time

Like you I would like to wipe the slate clean
Start all over, it isn't that easy
With each change we make
Each step we take towards that change
Life will start to get a little easier

As I have said once before
Take my hand
Take a pen
Talk to me, it can't do any harm

It can only help

Thursday, 30th May 2013 - Questions?

I started off wanting to ask questions, I also want answers, but, I know that only I can give answers, because it is my life and slowly things will unravel:-

I want to ask the questions
Why do I feel so low
Why does it have to be me
Why doesn't anybody understand
Why can't I believe?

What do you think they will say to me next
What do you think they would say if they knew
If they knew I was depressed would they tell me to snap out of it
I only wish I could
I sit and tell myself just to snap out of it

When I am sat smiling and happy
I think that it has all gone away, but deep down I still have the feeling
The feeling of how my mood will change
Change from the smile on my face to tears in my eyes
I don't know what clicks inside, I only wish I did

I have watched myself go up and down, round and round
Not knowing if my head is coming or going
Some people can cope with their pasts
Some of just lucky enough to not have the pain
Nor the thoughts to remember

I just want to know how to use this past
Use it to help me
To help others set their lives back on track
To get in on the straight and narrow
To use it for my future

I said it only this afternoon
And wondered why I couldn't turn it around
I realised and I have to keep thinking this
For all that has happened in the past
I wouldn't be where I am now

I know that I wouldn't be hurting
But I also wouldn't be writing this post or poem
I wouldn't be trying to reach out, supporting others
Others who are in similar situations
Be it worse or better than me, I don't know, I don't care

As long as I am helping and supporting others
Then I am not worried
I am also helping myself.
I want the brick walls to smash
I want my words to break the barriers that sit between them and us

Questions don't matter
You have to have answers
Be honest and you will find someone
Someone else like me who will help you

All I say is don't forget, you never know when it will help someone else.

Thursday, 30th May 2013 - Dream a Dream

If I dream a dream it may help me to concentrate during the day:-

As I sit thinking on my own
I want to know the reasons why
Why this has all happened to me
Why my life couldn't have been straight forward
What it was that made my life the way it was

As I sat thinking this afternoon
It really hit me
There is a reason
A reason for everything happening
The pain in my past has helped me to get here

Where I am in love
I have a long term contract job
I live on my own
Where I have found my soulmate
When I know that my future can only get better

All I want to think is that there is someone who wants me
There is a place for me permanently
There is a pathway for me to walk
There is a sunlight to help me on the way
But, if you have never had these in your life it is difficult to think about it

I dream a dream
Where all of the above will become true
There is security in my life
This dream is positive thinking
It helps me to get through my day

Friday, 31st May 2013 - Pieces of the Picture

I would like to thank each one of you who have read my posts. I have started to fit my pieces into the picture and you will keep going, but, if you can help someone else pick up theirs along the way then all the better for you, it is one thing I say do not forget what you have been through, it will help you as it is starting to help me:-

As you walk along the road of shattered glass
You will pick up a piece at a time
It won't hurt you for long
Because you will place each piece
Back to where it belongs

You will turn around
Placing each shattered piece of pain
Back to where it was
Because when you have finished
The picture will be whole

Each time you place that piece
It will help you to deal with the pain
The hurt that you have been dealing with
You are putting it where it belongs
In your past, not your future

When each shattered piece is back in place
You will find that you can work on it
Working towards your future
You ask me how
That is down to you how it will help you

If you think for everything that has shattered
You are now strong enough to pick up the pieces
With this strength and each piece
You are putting back together your life
Making you a stronger person

Take a piece now in your hand
It could be the smallest piece of shard
That will still create what your future is going to be
The next time you pick up one, it is up to you when
Will help to put together the picture

This picture is one of your past and creating your future
Your past will help you build up your future
To become a stronger person
Every time to you pick up a piece your strength grows
You are becoming you again

Now you have the whole picture
Take a long hard look
See if you want your past
If you don't turn the picture around
You see a mirror

A mirror of yourself
A new you, someone stronger
Someone more beautiful
Someone who now has the strength to look into the future
And say this is me, each step I take is me

Don't ever forget who you are
If you do, look into that mirror
The reflection of that person is you
Turn it around and see where you have come from
Perhaps you will be able to help someone to pick their next piece up

Pick up a piece, look in the mirror to see you, then help someone else

Friday, 31st May 2013 - A New Dance with New Music

I can hear new music, music of my future not my past, this doesn't mean that I can't hear the old music, some days it is louder than the new music and my feet do keep going to it, but, I know it will stop the more I learn and trust the new music and dance: -

Can you hear the music playing
Listen to it in the distance
It is sad
It is moving further and further away
Getting slower and slower

As you walk on
The sound will get softer and softer
It will stop soon as you start moving closer
Closer to the music that is beckoning you
Welcoming you onto the dance floor

As you take one step
You see the lights shining on you
Look behind you
As you stop hearing the other music,
The music of your past is stopping as the new one starts

There are others around you
Holding your back and wanting to teach you
Teach you how to dance
Dance to the new music
The steps will be difficult, but, we are patient

You keep looking back
As you see some people disappear
People you need to let go of
So that you can learn this new dance
The music starts your toes tapping

We will start with simple steps
Baby steps, so you can remember how it goes
So that you can dance on your own
With the new people in your life
To be able to help let go of the pain of the past

Leave behind people who have hurt you
Leave the pain behind you
Not to forget it, because it can't be
But, you will look toward the new dance
You will enjoy the new steps more

See the new light shining down on you
Trust the new people teaching you
Hear the beats to the music
Feel the new step in your feet
Beam the fresh smile on your face and the stars in your eyes.

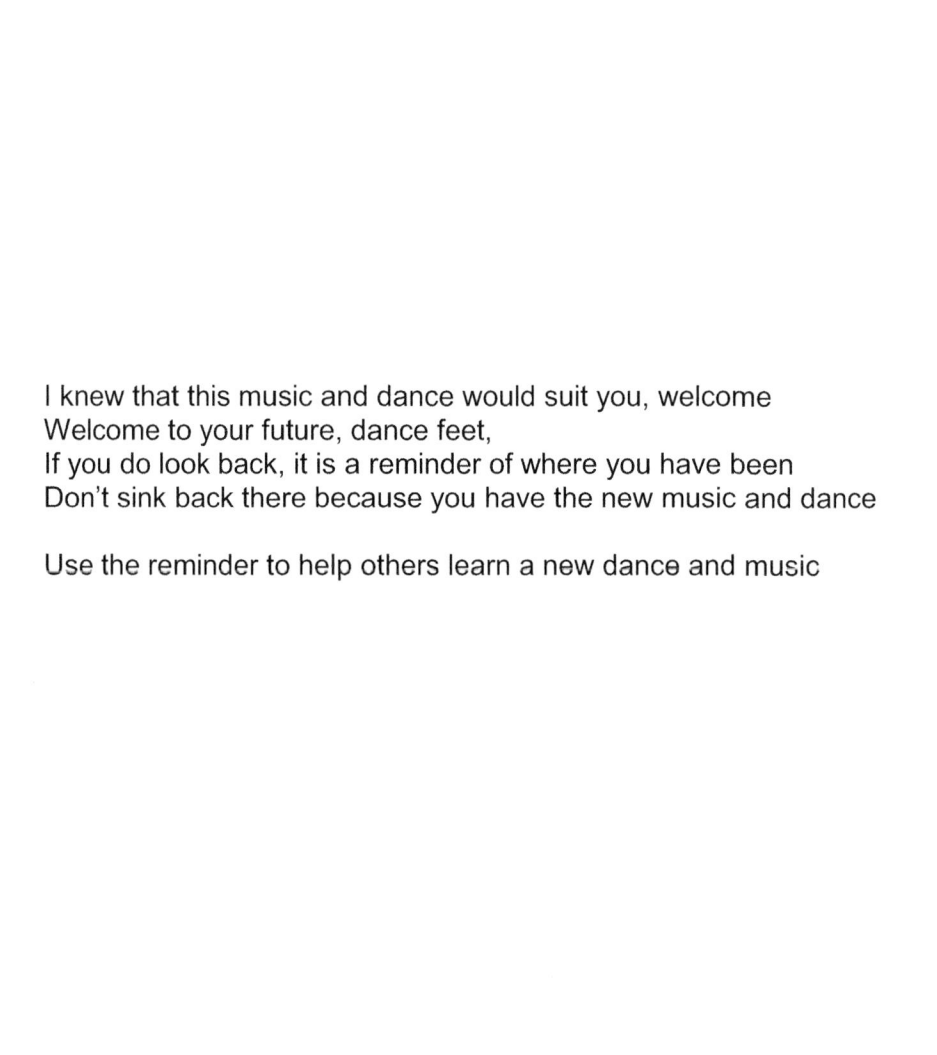

I knew that this music and dance would suit you, welcome
Welcome to your future, dance feet,
If you do look back, it is a reminder of where you have been
Don't sink back there because you have the new music and dance

Use the reminder to help others learn a new dance and music

Friday, 31st May 2013 - Hello, Beautiful Person

Let the tears roll, there are so many of us who have friends who say exactly what I am saying in my poem today, they are all crying quietly for us, because we don't see our own strength and how amazingly beautiful each one of us is, don't shake your head, which is what I did as I wrote this poem and I can feel the tears welling up now as I can hear my support saying the same to me read and see what you think:-

I am crying
Because you can't see what you are
Come out of the dark
Don't shuffle along on your bum
Stand up and turn around

I want to see you
Okay don't
But, the way you are talking
You are a beautiful person
I don't need to see you

I want you to see the person
The person I see deep inside of you
I want you to love you
Not just to hear what I am saying
To listen and see what I see

A beautiful, amazingly strong person
Look how far you have come
Look what you've got ahead of you
You can only make it if you see what I see
If you can see what is in there, inside you

It shines out of you
Other people can see it
I know where you are
Unless you make the next step
You won't get to where you want to go

It doesn't matter what has happened in the past
It will dull with pain
It won't leave you alone, it will just help you to support others
You will become more brilliant and beautiful than you are now
Your strength will just grow

Friday, 31st May 2013 - Many thanks

My vote of thanks to people who I don't know, but, know me:-

How do I thank so many people
People whom I don't know,
But, do know me only because of my writing
You have made me feel so good
And kept my strength up for writing

How do I get to know who you are
I don't, but, all I can say is that I am so grateful
You have given me the strength
Through this rough time
I'm not stopping, I just want to give you thanks

This is a vote of appreciation
For those who have read my good poems
And some of my not so good ones
Hopefully you will carry on hearing me
Supporting you and myself through poetry and posts

Once again Thanks

Friday, 31st May 2013 - You...

Aaargh well it goes like this, you know that every so often I get to a soppy poem, just to say a massive thank you to the person who is supporting me, it may not have anything to do with mental health, as I was thanking my readers, I had to thank my biggest supporter for all that he has done. So here goes:-

You have given me what I have asked for
What I have asked for all my life
To be able to live the way I want to
Not the way that you want me to

You have let me think how I have always wanted to think
Thinking clearly and freely is what I have always asked for
You have taken down the bars from my mind
Allowing me to think my way and not yours

You have let me see what I wanted
It doesn't matter how much or little
To be able to see the things I have always wanted to see
Letting me see the colours and the beautiful things around me

You have told me what I what I wanted to hear
Not what I have asked for
What you wanted to tell me
It is what I have been waiting to hear the whole of my life

My ears now listen to the things around me
Someone has taken the cotton wool out
To hear the things that you have to say
I can hear the new music to the new dance with you and the World

You have taken the binds from my legs
My feet can now move to help my new dance
They hear the new music
As they beat like they have never done before

You have set my heart free
It was so tied up before
Now, it is free and pumping

Enough to love you and everything else around me

Friday, 31st May 2013 - Deep Inside

Inside me and inside you:-

Look at what you can find
Look deep down inside
You may be shocked at what is there
It will be what people have told you is there for a long time

Below the dark place
Behind the solid heart
Under the skin
Chip away at the stone encasing your heart

If you can do this
You may have the strength
To find what is hiding
To hide what you keep finding

Come on find what is in there
If you can't find it now
Look for it later
It will be there

It might take time
It might be hard work
You will find it, if you believe it
One day they will both happen.

You will find what is hiding

You will hide what you keep finding

Saturday, 1st June 2013 - Amazingly Strong

I get told what is in this poem so many times, I just never have the courage to follow it through:

Why is it I can't see beyond what is on the surface
I can only see what is on my skin
Not under it
I can only see the things that don't matter

Why can't I see what you see
The strength that you say I have
My beauty for which I cannot see
How amazing I am, I wish I knew as I am only me

Why don't I have the belief you have
The faith you have in me is so strong
But, I can't see how
Because all I see is an empty shell

You turn me around and look in the mirror
Asking me to tell you what I see
I see nothing but a human being
Someone who has been ravaged by pain and hurt

I look at you as you stand behind me holding tight
You whisper in my ear
That pain has got me to where I am now
The pain inside is my strength

As you wipe a tear from my face
You tell me that the tear is my beauty
The beauty wanting to shine out
Shunning the pain and helping my strength

You tell me that the faith you have in me
Is the belief to know that I will dance again one day
Dance to the new music I have started to hear
And stop listening to the old music

You whisper how I am free now
Free to let go of what is hurting
Let my strength grow even more
Letting my amazing beauty shine even more

You tell me that I am going to do good
Great things,
My writing will bring out things for others
That I will keep helping others in ways unknown

So here I am trying to pluck up the courage
To say that I am the beautiful person
Amazingly strong
Trying to write what good and experience I have to help both you and I

I want you to be amazingly strong
Do something different day
Even if it is taking a step outside the door

This takes all the strength you can muster, that is courage my friend

Saturday, 1st June 2013 - Taking the Time

I have been on the go for a long time without relaxing, the pain hurts, I now need to take a step back and realise that all of me needs to relax and take perspective of what is going on around me.

I can hear my music
But, my feet don't want to dance today
The music is beautiful
So are the words to the song
The lights are so bright

The lights are blinding me
I just want to go back into the dark
If I take one more step
perhaps that would be better
Just one step forward

I have know in myself there is nothing wrong
With taking that one step back either
To take reflection of the past
Put the future into perspective
So I don't miss the right way to go

I need to stop
I am walking and dancing to fast
The music needs to slow
The words need to soften
And the lights need to be turned down

I feel a hand on my back to guide me
Someone else is taking my hand in theirs
As the music slows
A hand that I trust as they hold me I feel trust
I feel support

There is a hand in my other hand
They are whispering in my ear
Telling me what I want to hear
Not just wanting but needing to hear
As the tears roll down, I slow down

The music is a hum
I can hear myself think
I can talk to someone
I must learn to slow down
That my music can be turned down

The dance can be slowed
To a pace that we can take
Take the time to think about things around you
The time you need to find perspective

The time for your body, mind and soul to relax

Sunday 2nd June 2013 - Today My Way

I have spoken before about taking that step back and today is that one day for me, to be able to think about today and today alone, not tomorrow or what is going to happen because I need time for me:-

Today
Yesterday
The day before
Next week
Next Month

Just days
With different names
It is still 24 hours
24 hours that could be painful

The days could be long
The nights very dark
Last week is your past
Don't forget it, but you have to pass it

Next week
Is too far away
Tomorrow
Will take too long

Today
Is what I need to think about
How to get through the day
Not to sit and think about all that has happened

Now
I am writing
The only way I know I can help me today
The steps I have taken are too much in the future

I need to take a step back
To think and reassess what I have done
Take things into perspective
To remain calm

I want to sit with my head in my hands
And sigh with today
Thinking of what is going to happen next
I can only hear people telling me what to do

Today
Is my day
I am not thinking about tomorrow
Just today, my way, nobody else's!

Sunday, 2nd June 2013 - Tomorrow is Another Day

I want you to feel that tomorrow can be better than today, just let today happen first:-

I have struggled with the past
When the past is brought to me
It is painful and there is no blame to lay
What I can't see at the moment
Is a way past these painful days

As I watch the ticking of the time
I see that I can't walk the line
I wobble away
At the end of each working day
If I am at home it is during the day

The pain can sometime hit me
When it wants to, whenever it wants to find me
It could be one word
That just stops me from moving forward
There will be a day when I can put any of these pieces away

When I find a way of putting them into place
The picture will be so much bigger
It will be so much clearer
That this picture is one of my past
The past I will put behind me to lead me forward

I want people to understand
Understand that I am not a child to be comforted
I am an adult with problems of trying to move forward
Until they understand I am nothing to them
I have nothing for them to hear unless they want to listen

There I people I know who say
They understand
But, haven't actually heard me
It can be a word from their sentence that takes me back
Back to the past I wish to forget

I am one person
There is only me
I am the manager of my life
And how it wants to roll
Roll down life's road no matter what bumps there are

I am at one of life's bumps
I know that if I pick up a piece
I will become stronger
I am going to get over this bump
But only with the people I want

As the pieces of the past face me
I face it and pick it up
As the piece gets fitted into the picture
It stops the pain, the hate and see the ugliness
The strength in each piece is amazing

They slot into place one by one
Now you know you have the strength
To get past that piece in the puzzle
Dry the tears for it
Stand up straight and smile even for just one second

As you stand there
You can take the next step to the piece ahead
And start again
Until you have a full picture
You can then reverse it

As you turn it you can see
See what the future holds
The beauty is finally shining out of you
You see what everyone else sees
Sees what is inside of you, because it is also on the outside

As you wander down the road
You will find that you want to look back
You can turn that mirror around and see it
You can look at the past and nod
That is what has made my future, it hurts but not so much

I know this because
I have picked up a piece and felt the strength
Just because you have a bad day
Doesn't mean you won't carry on tomorrow
Tomorrow is another day, one that you can pick another piece

Find Peace for today and live for tomorrow after all it could be a better day

Sunday, 2nd June 2013 - Live It!!

I want you to hear part of what has made me write this blog and the way I am today:-

I have been bullied for far too long
By different people
Different friends
Even family in my lifetime
That I am not going to take it anymore

There are only a two people
Two people who can tell me what to do
That is me and my manager
No man or woman has any right
No right to take control or manage me

I wouldn't be where I am now
I would be more free
I know that if it wasn't for my past
I wouldn't have this future

I also have to be able to manage me
Manage my own life
Not let someone take me over
Or take over me
I want you to hear me whoever you are

You may be going through the same thing
I walked out from the last man who did this to me
Who wanted to control me
Who stalked me to the end
Who drove me to the destruction I am at now

I am finally starting to realise
That there are others who have helped
I know that I have been weak, too weak to realise
Now I have turned that around to my strength
I am taking it in hand

Don't let anyone get you down
This is your life and you only have one choice

Live it!

Sunday, 2nd June 2013 - Open up!

Open up on paper or by keyboard, let your fingers do the talking :-

I don't know how I am feeling
I will tell you this evening
I am having a numb feeling
One of excitement and then rage
I want to just be me

So I am sitting here and talking
Talking the best way I can
Writing this poem
I love writing because I can write what I like
I can tell you how I feel

Try it
It doesn't have to be a long verse
It can be short or however long you want
I find it is the best therapy
Along with listening to music

A bright beautiful day
A cool through draft
And I am writing away as I want to
This is the way today will go
I want this day to go after all this is my day off

Open up to your keyboard
It may take a few times before you feel better
If you can't talk, write it
Let it all out
Get it all on the screen

Pick up the pieces slowly
Then you will become a stronger person
piece by piece you let the past go past
You can walk on to the next or take a rest
You will have people around you to help you

I thank the World I have someone to lean on
Someone who supports me
Someone who holds my hand
Who talks to me
But, what I can't say is what I write

All I ask is you try it, if you want to leave a verse put it in the comments

Sunday, 2nd June 2013 - Dream a Dream

I always dream a dream - it may not always be good, but, this is how I feel about it:-

I dream a dream
That one day I will see
See what others see
The light beyond the darkness
The freedom beyond the bars

I had a dream
That all I could see was silence
No words spoken
And a darkness enveloping me
As the bars stabbed through my heart

I found a dream
It was covered in white fluffy clouds
With a shimmer of lighting covering me
I was too scared to reach out and touch
I felt imprisoned by the people who did not understand

I heard a dream
One of which there was new music
People who wanted to teach me a new dance
Something to help the silence from the old music
My feet have only just tapped to this

I will live a dream
Where I will learn to trust the teachers of my new dance and music
This will help the light to open my eyes
To lift me to touch the skies where the bars have lifted to
Setting my heart free from the hurt of the pain once lived

You too can have a dream, close your eyes

Sunday, 2nd June 2013 - Caterpillar to Butterfly

You and I will change to the butterfly with a little help from the others in our new lives, face to face, online communities or our workplaces have a read and see:-

Have you ever thought....
How your life could have been different
If any of this hadn't have happened in the past
If you didn't have any of the Mental Health conditions
No matter how small or how big it is

Have you ever thought....
What would have happened
If you life had changed
If you had done just one thing differently
Would your life had changed

Or would you rather you did what you did
Are you pleased that you made the mistake you made
Would you be where you are if you had
If only, if only you keep saying
But, would you have learnt what you know

I know I wouldn't
If I had met my other half back then
I would never have got to where I am now
I would never have the experience in work or relationships
I would have been young and naive, he would never have me as I am

I know to you
What I am asking is mad
But, is it?
Sit back and think about it
Sit down and think would I have learnt anything

I am asking you
Because as you pick up the pieces and put them back together
The pain you are feeling and trying to take away
Is giving you the strength to learn and move on
Move on with your experience and past

It is giving you the chance to change
Learn whatever you have to learn
I know that I am learning
As I piece together the picture of my past
And I am growing stronger as I do it

Knowing one day
I will come out of the chrysalis like the butterfly
I would change from the caterpillar I am now
To a beautiful inside and out amazingly strong butterfly
I will be able to fly to the sky and touch it with my colourful wings

Monday, 3rd June 2013 - Who Am I?

Wanting to tell people who I really am underneath:-

Today the music wasn't playing
My feet weren't dancing
I felt like I was stood on the dance floor alone
Nobody stood around me

I couldn't wait until I got home
I could see everyone around me
Walking and talking past me
But wasn't listening or seeing them

I wanted to hear what they said
But, I couldn't
My head was all fuzzy
I don't want to tell anyone

I am walking with my head held high
I am talking normally
I am relaxing
What am I doing wrong

What is it about me that is strange
Why can they not see the beauty inside
Perhaps they can and I am being silly
That is what I keep telling myself

I want someone to walk up to me
When I am really low and ask if I am alright
For me to say "No"
For them to then ask what is wrong

One day before I leave
I will tell them what I have done
That I got through all these months
Hiding without one of them knowing who I really am

This is what people miss
When they don't understand
The person below the surface as they shun you aside
It's not down to me if they want to push me aside

Monday, 3rd June 2013 - Good Night, One and All

Well, I thought about having a plain simple poem as I sit drinking the glass of wine this evening: -

I can hear the evening sky
See the setting of the sun
As I close my eyes
The birds song carries on

I can see the fields stretched out in front of me
The music from the room below
I can watch the glowing colours
From the evening flow

Open your ears and listen
What can you hear this eve
I bet it isn't as beautiful as I can see
I wonder if they are singing just for me

This is the last month within this room
As I listen to the birds in the sky
With the green trees and stone walls
I wish I wish it was me who could fly

I want to sit here all the day
Listen to the sounds that surround me
Watch the changing ways
I have seen the snow, the rain and the beautiful glow

I know it will soon be time to say good night
But just before I go
I will hear a Tawny twit twoo
Even watch the moon and the stars rise high

The very last thing I want to say
Is have a peaceful evening wherever you are
Close your eyes and hear the sounds
Watch the colours all around

Good Night One and All!

Tuesday, 4th June 2013 - Looking in the Mirror

I have been talking to my counsellor today and she has told me what she thinks, let's see:-

Have you taken a look in the mirror
Are you scared of what you are going to look at
Do you not want to know what you are going to see
Would you rather leave it to someone else
To tell you what you look like?

I will tell you
I have taken a long walk today
By doing what I can't do usually
That is talk about my past
Or what is happening now to a stranger

I have had to take a good, hard long look
At someone I don't know
Someone I do want to know
I could see what was happening
I took a step nearer to another piece

That piece is going to be one I will be proud of
One I will move past
I took a step nearer to being positive
About me
Wanting to find out who me was

I looked and stared and glared
I was told how much I have done
It won't necessarily cure me
It will help me
It is something that will help me be me

This what we in the dark
Are all aiming for isn't it
Seeing the light of positivity
I don't care how long
My pride was touched by the fact I am on the right road

I know there will be more to do
A lot more
But, I also know that you are with me
I may not know me
But, just reading these helps me to help you

I support you and you support me
The pride shines out of my heart
If you can just put a piece in the picture
The one that is going to be nicer than your past

You too will be able to look in the mirror.

Tuesday, 4th June 2013 - Come on Out

I thought I would finish the day with this one for those who love the country:-

Take a look at the colours around
Have you seen them lately
The colours that are so natural
Or are you still blinded by the sight of black
Take a peek from under there, come on out

There are the yellow and black bees and wasps buzzing
They help make the pollen
Of the purple wisteria climbing the houses
With the beautiful sandy coloured stone
Which are shaded by the beautiful green leaved trees

The grey roads
That are surrounded by the green hedgerows
Which are surrounding the beautiful golden rapeseed
The harvest that is growing for the next month or so
The times we look away and yet black is all around

Black is such a good colour of nature
So is brown of the turned over fields that the farmer has ploughed
The blue of the lakes that can be held in the old quarries
Which is followed by the reds, blues, greens and gold of the birds
They are singing their hearts out through the day and night

Have you seen the hills that roll over the countryside
The ones that in the winter are covered in white
In the spring are green
And the summer covered by the golden light of the sun
In the Autumn, covered by beige and reds for the trees and harvest

As the night light starts to fall
The stars brighten the sky
With the moon shining down
Casting a silver light over the colourful landscape
Look out tonight and you will see

Have a nice evening and look out your window from the dark

Wednesday, 5th June 2013 - Cutting It Short!!

A day with a migraine where I have had to lay in a very dark room with tablets as well:-

Very dark and muzzy day
With a head to match
So dull on a bright day like this
A feeling of nausea
And being sick

My day has been full of not sure where I am
I won't keep you long
Because I can't stay long
The darkness is calling me as I can't take the light
My eyes are crying because my head is hurting

I haven't had this in a very long time
But I know I should be fine soon
Thank you one and all for looking in
I will be back tomorrow night
When I am at home.

Good night again and sorry to cut it short!

Thursday, 6th June 2013 - Not Understood!!

I am still poorly today have been sleeping all day from the migraine yesterday and have a swollen eyelid on both eyes:-

I sometimes feel like I am being pushed out
As if nobody worries about me
Nobody cares about my feelings
Change is good for everyone,
But, not when you need it little by little

I feel like everyone wants to see what I am doing
That they need to control and see what I am doing
I know it may not be meant that way
But, that is how I feel

I feel like I am pushed into a corner
So that everyone watch
Like feeding time at the zoo
Just in case I put a foot wrong
Just in case I am seen to be alright

I don't need to be watched
It is as if I am being controlled
As I have done before
They can't see that I am writing
Needing time to myself

I will hide if it is needed
I will stay away
I have to have privacy
I sit in an open office in front of people
They are watching all day, I need to scream

I don't know what to do
It keeps happening every week
They can't get it that I need my space without talking
They keep talking to me when I need some time to me
What can I do?

Where do I go?
Do I go and sit back in the bedroom on my own
It feels like she thinks I am taking him away from her
I am not and would never do that
We need time as well

I need time to be on my own
I need space
Space to put my legs down
Space for me to think
Quiet to think

It will never be understood

Thursday, 6th June 2013 - My Dream One Day

I have read something somewhere today that has made me think about this and my dream for my future and I hope it may help with yours, for the pain you are feeling now is a strength not a weakness:-

I can feel the pain
But I can understand what it is
It is just the being strong enough
Strong enough to get past it
Strong enough to pick up the pieces

Those pieces one day
When I have put them back together
Will make a picture
A picture that I will like
One that will help me to look back

When I can look back I will be able to smile
Smile at the history
The history and past that has helped me
To get to where I am today
Where I will be when I have learnt to get past it

I will be me
I will have all the strength that I have never had before
Something that will help me walk by
Instead of crying at the reminders
I can smile and laugh them past

That will be my strength one day!!
It is my dream

It is my music and my new dance!!

Friday, 7th June 2013 - How Do I Stop?

I wish that I could say that my day has gone well, but, I can't and won't lie to you because if I lie to you I am lying to myself and I will never get out of this:-

How do I stop
Stop thinking people are talking behind my back
Thinking they are being horrible
Thinking that I am a horrible person
When actually they aren't

Why have I got such a low esteem
That I am worrying about what somebody says
About me
I was off sick
Does it matter what they think or say

I am going to change myself
I am going to go into work
With my head held high
Keep quiet and head down
Make a laugh when I can

I want to stop feeling paranoid
I want to feel confident again
I have had so many years of being like this
I don't want to feel like it again

I want to hold my head up high
I want to have the strength
To have the confidence
To carry on with work
The dull dark corner a picture of the past

I want to see the light of day
To see the sunshine through the clouds
The rain blown away by the wind
I want to feel like the old me

I want to dance again.

Friday, 7th June 2013 - I Am Sorry

Oh, I wish I could pick myself up today, but, I can't I'm sorry :-

I am sorry
I am sorry for anyone who knows me
Anyone who thinks I am normal
Someone who thinks I can be normal
Normal is not being strange

I am strange
I am sorry I am
But, I am sure you wouldn't have me any other way
What way would you have me
What is normal

I am weird
Especially thinking you want me straight
I can't be
I'm not
I want to feel normal, I know I can't

I want my past to stop now
I want my future to be a fresh start
I know this won't happen
So I have to realise

I am going to be sorry for the rest of my life for being me

Friday, 7th June 2013 - Help Me as I Helped You

Every time I fall I feel like I need to start again, I know I don't but I want to ask for the help:-

What's wrong?
I want to dance
Dance the new dance
Do you remember the one
The one you started to teach me

What's happened?
I want to hear the music
The new music I started listening to
Do you remember
You started playing it to me last year

You took my hand
And helped me to understand
Understand that I could trust you
Trust you to teach me the new dance
Leave the old one behind

You led me to the dance floor
Into the limelight
Started the music slowly
Showed me a few steps
Helped me to trust you a little bit more

Whilst I was learning to trust you
I supported you
Showing you the new dance too
Helping you put the step to the new music
What you didn't know was that I was falling

As I fell I held you up
I showed you the dance in full
You learnt to trust that was the right dance
The music for you is nearly in full swing
Now you are having to bring me back

I trust you as I take your hand once more
I am starting to hear the music
But you are going to have to hold tight
So that I don't fall back
So that I keep my strength to carry on the dance

I want to hear the music too
I want my feet to dance
But you may have to show me it again
I have taken your hand
Now guide me, let me hear and my feet

Please help me I want to dance with you to the new music

Friday, 7th June 2013 - Listen To The New Notes

{lay a new song tonight or a song you know with a new singer feel the beat of the music and imagine where you're life could go. I have done it so many times today with a new album my support has given me it helped me to calm down. Listen to my words today:-

The notes keep playing
I keep listening
What a way to hear your new time ahead
I can see the lights
As the drum starts to beat

There are new faces around
New hands outstretched
Smiley faces around me
As the instruments start to play my song
The song I don't know the words to yet

What I want to know is which hand to take
Which one will be the first to help me
I still some old faces around
Some that have moved on with me
I turn to see the faces from the past

As I look to my past
The dancing stopped along time ago
The music kept playing with big dull thuds
Something I had never heard before
It has disappeared as I start to look ahead

The person who I first trusted
Is the person who has shown me a few steps
As I fallen back to my past before
I know you will pick me back up
But, this will happen with a little help from my friends

I can hear the notes playing
Am starting to hear the words to the song
As I dance around the floor with you
My friends faces will start to smile
I can feel their hands

The light is just glimmering
It will start to brighten
As will the night sky with the stars that are going to be shown me
When you show me one step
I will be able to take the next

Once word has been learnt
So will the next
Each step and word learnt
Will mean something to the next
It will also mean something to help with the pain from the past

As I feel the wind beneath my heels

The dance and song will get easier

Friday, 7th June 2013 - It Will Be Me Who Walks Away

I have a friend who doesn't understand or what to understand what I am feeling, they think that I can just snap out of it, there may be days that are normal and I am having a good day, they have never seen me in a bad you will hear from my poem what has happened:-

What do I say
How can I talk
I can't
Which is why I will walk
Walk away

I will walk away
If you don't understand
Because I can't explain
It is hard to explain something
You don't understand

Where do I start
When does it end
That you say you understand
Alas you don't at all
Even when I fall

All you know how to do is
Walk away
To shout and bellow
To not understand why
Why I have fallen

Just walk on by
I need someone who will listen
Someone who will hear what I say
Not someone shouting
Snap out of it

There are enough people
Who do that to me
I don't need friends like that too
Listen and hear what I say
You will understand

If not I am the one who will walk on by

Leaving you behind

Friday, 7th June 2013 - For My Friend

This is a beautiful poem for my friend who's cat and best friend is poorly:-

A friend by my side for so long
She won't disappear
She will always be here in my heart
Always be around with me

No matter what happens
No matter what goes on
We both may hurt
We are always there for each other

I know the day we part
Will be the day the tears will fall
They will tear my heart away
But, I will love her always

She is there when I am alone
She is there when I am asleep
When nobody has been there to hear me
She is there

My beautiful friend
Thank you for being you

Friday, 7th June 2013 - To Infinity and Back

I have one last word to say tonight to the one person who loves me so much, so yes this is soppy, turn your heads, close your eyes I don't care or read if you dare:-

To Infinity and Back
That is me to you
You to me
I have waited for so long
So long to tell one person

I have never seen
Someone fall for me so quickly
Someone who trusts me
Someone who will open up to me
The time we have had together so far has been awesome

There have been hurdles for both of us
The hurdles that we are getting over
Things we learn about each other
But we are so together
We will never be apart

You have held my hand
Held onto me tight
You would never let me go
Your kiss, your laugh
Makes me weak at the knees

Every time I look into your eyes
I learn something knew
I see that you love me
You are such a beautiful and amazingly strong person
You are the one I will dance under the stars with.

When I have learnt my dance with you!!

Saturday, 8th June 2013 - Wake Up to Change

How often do you wish there was someone you could talk to at work?

How many of us say that nobody ever hears what I want them to say?

Are you in an office where times could be a little more flexible if your work was more understanding or you understood why the times had to be so strict?

If only someone could hear what I am saying I wouldn't be going deeper into this, I wouldn't feel so stressed, anxious or hate my job so much?

I wish the company just stood by me and helped me with my problems not just trying to push me down and making me feel lower?

I work for an American company, I'm not going to mention names because that would be unfair. I have been in and out of depression for most of my life and I am having to help myself. Taking home the problems I have during the day in fact they are twice as bad as when they started at the beginning of the day, if only I had spoken to someone at the start of the low mood it may not have fired into a really low mood to get home to the only one I can talk to and start of an angry mood.

If there had been someone who would understand me, someone on hand I could have talked about the problem to, perhaps a support group of some sort to enable me to say what I needed to say. If it was having a support network within the company, I don't care if I would have to make my time up at the end of the day or some other time, it is just having a telephone number within work that is open to everybody, not just permanent staff, also contract workers.

Permanent staff this is nothing against you, but, temp working is the hardest industry to be in, it is insecure, you don't know when the contract is going to end, where the next job is coming from, you want a permanent job, but, because you have been temp for so long you have forgotten what it is like to pass a permanent job interview. You get a contract, you wonder into a brilliant new company assignment then you find you are in the same loophole again "You can't do that because you are a contractor" or "You can't join in because you are a contractor"

What I am asking for is ALL employers of ALL companies no matter how small or large to look at the number of staff who do or may have depression, human beings who need a network of help to talk to or one person to go to who understands with a listening ear, because sometimes that is all we need a listening ear for half an hour even five minutes or just some time to pull ourselves together if we had understanding companies, but this is for ALL staff not just for permanent staff.

I want to shout this from the rooftops because I AM in a Depression, one I have to work through, if companies had help it may be that there maybe more people working through depression not just sat at home hoping to get better.

I am sorry I will come back down from my soap box, all I am asking if there are any bosses, employers or managers who are hearing what I am saying, we are not asking for anything different to anyone except to be heard in the workplace and understood by someone, to be understood by you, to have no prejudices against people with depression.

How many agree that if they had this kind of network support or someone in work they could turn to it would help?

Let's help raise the stigmatism of Mental Health, Help me make this step and change today. Unless your boss knows how can it change.

Saturday, 8th June 2013 - Me

I love being at home, but, because I can't tell people what my problem is it is where everything comes out which has got to be horrible for my partner, I cry at home, I scream at home, I get angry at home yet, I just want to talk to someone please read about me:-

My darkest place is at home
What I want is to be able to say something
Something that will help lift all stigma
Stigma that has stuck for so long
That nobody wants to talk about it

I want to talk about it though
So do you
And you and you
If you stay quiet
It will never be spoken about

It is down to you to have to lift this as well
You need to talk out loud to someone
Tell people it isn't all in your mind
It is here in your heart as well
I DO know how you feel

I have been through
Three broken marriages
Countless amounts of abuse
Both physical and mentally
I have no family nearby all mine have moved away

So if you think you are the only one
You aren't
I am starting to talk about my problems
I have had to leave friends behind
Also family who have caused me too much pain

I have had to learn to help
Support someone else before I got to mine
I have given in finally to realising
That this is not just going to go away
I do what I have to

I write instead of making a speech
I stand on my soap box, when I type
To a lot of you who think this is difficult
It isn't because I can get what I want to say
On a screen and talk to all around me

I want to help you
As well as helping me
I want you to be heard
I want to be understood
Someone to finally listen to what I am saying

To be able to see past the sad face
So I can see past the darkness
I can hear past the silence
Feel the touch of a friendly hand
I want you to be you and me to be me

Saturday, 8th June 2013 - Hear & See Me

I can't see anything sometimes when I am at work, I can't hear what is going on around me it is all muffled, I would like to ask an employer just once to hear what I have to say, I do contract work for a living, so I am going from place to place, but, I never get the same benefits like talking to a counsellor because I am not permanent, also there are not always these facilities for their staff:-

Can you see
That the darkness
That dark Corner
Their crying behind the curtains
That is all they can see

Can you hear
What they are listening to
The sounds inside their heads
The muffling of voices
They can't hear much else

Can you feel
The numbness inside
The anger and the lowness
The despair inside their minds
That is all they feel

That is how I feel
If you don't listen
If you don't want to help
There is nobody else
Only those at home

I am here in another place
Wanting someone to hear me
To understand what I say
If only there was someone
Someone to talk to about this

I just need to talk for a few minutes
I will make it up sometime during the day
Just give me sometime so that I can talk to someone
I need an ear to listen to me
To understand so I can get back to work

I don't want to sit here day after day
Feeling like this
If you made it easier by just having one person
Even one person to hear me
I would come back

If you could make it easier by being flexible
I could work to whenever I wanted
I would work as hard as possible
Don't let me slip away
You know I work hard

All I ask is you hear what I say
So I can go back to work

Saturday, 8th June 2013 - Nobody wanted to listen to Me

I have been out for the evening, it was nice to be out but:-

Have you ever got agitated with people
For looking at you
They talk about something near your problem
Then skip around it
Like the elephant in the room

Have you ever got agitated
When the end of the evening is coming near
You are starting to feel uncomfortable
Because still they want to say something
But they don't, feeling like the elephant in the room

I was the one without the problem
The problem nobody wanted to face me with
The problem wasn't there
I wanted to talk about it
I wanted to say why

Being in a group of people isn't easy
As you will know
It is very difficult
They wouldn't even talk to me about my writing
They couldn't even touch the subject

They only just got to talking about me
It felt like I shouldn't have even been there
I was part of the group but not
I sat and tried to hear what everyone said

Nobody wanted to listen to me

Sunday, 9th June 2013 - Talk to Me (Not a Poem)

Do you know how it feels to be ignored by people?

For them not to talk about your past just in case they start some sort of emotion off?

I am talking about a different kind of stigma today one that all of you know too well, where friends, family or strangers even, who know that you are depressed dare not speak to you about things in your life just in case it sets your emotions off, yet what they don't realise is avoiding or ignoring them or you is worse than talking about it.

I want to reach out to everyone today to talk to someone, I dare you to reach out,talk to them face to face or lift up the telephone to a depression sufferer no matter what level high or low and actually ask "How are you feeling today?" because a lot of us will not just break down in tears some of us will feel good just for the fact someone is asking us out loud, knowing someone is hearing us, someone is talking about how we really feel.

Do you really know how it really feels for someone to ask that? It feels like you are hearing that we have depression, you are understanding there is something wrong, if the conversation carries on to talking about things, then let them talk or if you want to ask them about what is happening because you don't understand and in the future instead of sitting in silence you have got past what you think is an "awkward moment" because you don't know how to talk to them when all we want is normality.

I am serious try it when you next see someone, someone who has told you or you know as a depression or Mental Health sufferer, it is easy really.

Mental Health has been behind closed doors for far too long and it is time for us to let it out, for us to make it known we are just normal human beings wanting to work, rest and play as anybody else does, we can do these things, we don't have to be labelled or shunned as abnormal, it is time we brought this to the forefront instead of left behind closed doors.

As a depression sufferer for many years, I have sat behind closed doors because a) I have been with people who don't realise that I am suffering from it or choose to be ignorant of it because they don't understand and b) Because I was with people who don't wish to know me behind the depression or even know about my depression without saying you need some pills or snap out of it what is up with you today. I don't understand everything of what is happening, all I can say is I AM A DEPRESSION SUFFERER, I have been for years.

I will stand or sit if you wish here until at least one person asks you or me how I actually am and realise that we do not make scenes we just need to talk about it, otherwise we suffer in silence as we have for many years.

Thank you for listening to Heartily Mindful A DEPRESSION SUFFERER and writer

Sunday, 9th June 2013 - Walking on Eggshells

This is a follow on from the article I wrote this morning, it is how I am feeling today, like people are walking on eggshells :-

What won't you talk to me
What is it that makes you stop
You were about to ask me
Or you want to ask me
Then you stop

I have problems like anybody else
Just unable to deal with them
Their way
I have had this on and off in my lifetime
Which is far too long

If you offered to even talk about them
It may help
You may know a way I can get around this
Instead of snap out of it
Chill or take a pill

Talking to someone like me
Can ease their pain
It may be the one moment
That they need to pick up a piece
A piece that makes them stronger

By that I mean
Their confidence in social
Talking to you without waffling or silence
They can hear their own voice at the moment
Because nobody will talk with them

Even if they don't want to talk
Reach out to them and show that you are there
That you care
You are feeling for them whatever it is
That is all they need to know

There are so many different ways
Ways you can help this person
Someone who needs someone to hear them
Understand them
You never know how this may change them

Listen to what they are saying to you
If you don't understand
Hear them
Don't just walk away
Keep trying

Sunday, 9th June 2013 - I Will One day

This is an old poem I wrote over a year ago on 16th May 2012, So you can see how slowly this feeling has been going on and off, and Now I am lucky enough to have a few of these things, but, I also realise now that it is time to let go and it is also going to take time to let the past go by, however I have that someone now to help and understand me not just to tell me to snap out of it :-

I will one day have a nice strong pair of arms around me
Those arms will hold me tight and never let go
They will let me hold them
They will make me laugh
Most of all they will help me love

I will one day have a warm heart to love someone
A heart that will beat faster and faster
A heart that someone will love back for me
A heart that is soft and gentle
We will love each other

I will one day have someone who will say no
Someone I can talk to
Someone with a voice of their own
Someone who enjoys what I enjoy
That someone is out there

I will one day hold my head up high
I will get through it
It will take time
It won't be easy
Now I have said goodbye to the past it is one step closer to the future

Monday, 10th June 2013 - Decision Making Day

I have had a day of hard thinking, discussions and perhaps a few results:-

Today has been a difficult day
It has been a hard thinking day
One that has taken me a step closer
Closer to being able to take time
Time to help me

Today has taken a hard knock
It was difficult to come to my conclusion
I didn't know what everyone was going to say
My other half realised that I need time out
Before I have to take time out

I have realised today that not everyone is the same
That there are people willing to listen
It is tiring thinking and talking
Discussing with others what you want to do
And realising that you may be able to achieve

I have only told part of the truth
Because I feel unable to tell all of the truth
As I feel I will lose my contract
One day I will be able to stand up
And say I have got through this depression

I will get through it
I may feel alone at the moment
But, I know I will get through this
I will help others

This will be the last time

Monday, 10th June 2013 - A Beautiful Drive Home

I have given you a picture of my drive home so peaceful and calm the total opposite to my day, with it I bid you a fond good night:-

As I drive with the wind
To get home to my room
I can see the bright yellow Laburnums as I pass
With the Wisteria over hanging the windows too

I drive past the trees
Of beautiful and different greens
Who would believe what is to be seen
On an greyish evening like this

As I wind down the grey windy roads
The air has a very slight chill
With the Wood Pigeon cooing
And the other birds singing to their hearts content

As I get nearer to the cottage
Stood in the middle of nowhere
I see brown fallow fields
Alongside the brightly coloured rape fields

As I get to the dusty dirt track
I can see the sun shining through the dark cloud
Waiting for me to go home
So I can say good night

I sit in my room
awaiting the beautiful sounds
One of the Tawny Owl
The other is still the cooing of the Wood Pigeon

With the chirping and singing of the little brown birds
I offer you all a peaceful evening
One night you may sleep
Through the calm and tranquility.

Just close your eyes and picture my ride home

Good night!

Tuesday, 11th June 2013 - Stop Silence Behind Work Doors

As you can see that my day has not been great, if only I had been able to talk to someone first thing this morning, I would not have been so agitated, confused or frustrated and been able to support my partner who is getting better from his breakdown when I got home:-

What a confusing and frustrating day
A day where things could have been so much clearer
One that if someone had actually stopped and asked
How are you?
Instead of I know you're okay, how are you?

I just needed to answer
With, not great
Instead I painted on a smile and went on
I wanted to scream
So much was going through my head!

Too much to think about
I wanted someone to sit me down
Or for me to have time out
To sit and think through what I was thinking about
Instead I sat there slowly going through my work!

I wanted to talk
If there had only been a chance
A chance to pick up the phone
Talk to someone who understood
Instead I was getting confused and frustrated

I wanted to think about my work as well
But, I couldn't not straight
I had to ask for some help
If only there had been someone
Who could have given me five minutes

This person didn't have to be a counsellor
Just someone who understood me
Understood what I was going through
I am a contractor so there is no chance of this
Because contractors can't use that service

I would like to have a work place
One that took care of contractors as well as permanent
Even taking care of all of them
To be able to have a network
One that will speak to someone when they need it

An employer who doesn't care
Doesn't care about what Mental Health problem you have
Because they have something or someone in place
One day this will happen
One day it will be realised that it makes the workplace easier

I want to go to my next employer
Let them tell me that they have someone to talk to
Someone who I can go to at anytime if I just need to shout or talk
I know this is a dream, perhaps a fantasy
But, it will happen and it will be before I retire!

Employers hear what I say
Please listen
For all employees to have someone to talk to
All in all I have a low day, if only I could have talked to someone
I may have been able to help support my partner when I got home!

Hear me when I say it needs to change for everyone
Silence is not good enough anymore!

Tuesday, 11th June 2013 - You Won't Close Another Door

iI am so fed up of hiding behind closed doors about who I am, what I am and how I am. I have my days of great intent and you will see throughout my poems and posts that they have their own waves of change. At the moment I want people to hear what is wrong with me, not just to hide behind closed doors, to actually hear what I have to say and I don't care who it is:-

Don't shut the door
I hate closed doors
It feels like something is being hidden from me
I feel enveloped in silence
Where I have been so many times before

Look at me
Watch my eyes as you close that door again
And again, you will see the sadness
The only voice I can hear is me
One of the only voices I hate hearing scream

Listen inside my head
You will hear the confusion
As yet another door closes
Because you aren't hearing me
You are only hearing you talking

You are now shouting at me
Asking what I want to hear
I want to hear my voice talk to you
Talk to you about the confusion and pain
Confusion and pain inside my head

It hurts more days than not
That is why I can't concentrate
That is why I am confused
The pain is still there because I can't talk about it
I write instead

Hear what I have to say and you may understand
It may help you to hear what I am going through
I am not ill
I have depression, a Mental Health condition
I am admitting it for all the World to hear

Because I am having the courage
The courage to stand up and be heard
That there is nothing wrong with a Mental Health illness
I have found the strength to admit I have something wrong
That I need to put myself back together

I want to hear it from behind other closed doors
I want others voices to be heard
Out loud, not quietly
There are days I want to take my own life
I have enough support not to

I will be heard
You will listen
I just write it
So I will shout it
Loud enough for you to hear and understand

I HAVE A MENTAL HEALTH ILLNESS AND I WILL BE HEARD

Tuesday, 11th June 2013 - Country Drive

My drive home in the country so a lot you will know this is usually my way of saying good night one and all, sleep tight and I will write for you tomorrow with a fresh head and heart :-

Country roads take me home
Wow what an evening to be on them
To see a Red Kite take flight
Or maybe a Buzzard
I know I have seen a Muntjac Deer today
That was just as I was driving to work

I sometimes see a Barn Owl or two
I have even seen a Tawny on the way home
The beautiful shades of colours in the clouds
With which to be able to see these beautiful creatures
Even the shades of green which make them stand out

As I look at the road with a sparkle in my eye
Knowing that there will be fields of bright yellowy gold
Watching the Wisteria climbing the grey stoned houses
With the drives winding by them
Where the cars will be parked as they all come home

I see the farmers still out in their fields
Driving their tractors to make sure everything is safe for the night
The green leaves rustling on the trees and hedgerows
The brown of the earth that has been tilled only days before
With some more yellow on the other side

As I hear the cooing of the doves
And the clicking of the Robin
I understand that the day is coming to a close
As I hear the rest of the even song
So for those of you not so lucky to see all of this

Close your eyes and relax in tranquillity as I tell you it again.

Wednesday, 12th June 2013 - I Want to Tell You....

I believe in telling the truth and it wasn't far off from coming out today if it didn't come out in a roundabout way hear what I have to say:-

Shout it from the roof tops
Tell it in the papers
I nearly did today
One thing stopped me
Stopped me from telling all to one person at work

Because like most of us
I was scared
Scared of losing my contract if I did
Worried that if I told the truth
That I would end up with no contract at all

It has taken me enough time to realise
That I need time off
Time to help look support my other half
Look after his mum
But also look after me as well

If employers, including those who taken on contractors
Would take a look at their employees all of them
Step back and realise that something needs to be done
To stop this dreadful silence
One that scares people to talk to others

To what end will this stop
Because the doors get slammed in their faces about Mental Health
Employers want the truth to be told to them
It will only happen when we can tell the truth
The truth about how we are without being dismissed

The truth that we all want to tell you
If we weren't going to be told that we couldn't cope
Can't cope with our jobs
We would tell you
If there was someone there just so we could off load

Off load with anything
It is the knowing that someone is there to hear
Not, have to see
We would be able to tell you everything
I should know I DO HAVE DEPRESSION

I want to shout that I am on Fluoxetine
I want to tell you that I see a counsellor
I want to tell you that mine is to do with my personal life
I want to tell you that I can cope with my job
I want to tell you it would be easier knowing that there is a network of people

Most of all I want to tell you the truth
I HAVE DEPRESSION and I AM Doing my job!!

Wednesday, 12th June 2013 - What Do I Do?

I don't want you to see this
The smile I paint on everyday
I want to allow the tears to come out
I don't want to have to leave until I get home

I want to be able to break down
In public wherever I want to
Even just for a few minutes
I want you to be able to hold me

I don't want you to ask me what is wrong
I want you to hold me
I want you to hold me and know why
I have cried for such a long time in silence

I have broken my heart in silence
Behind closed doors
I want to cry until all my tears have gone
I know that will be a while

What I don't know what to do
Is what to say when you don't understand
That's what scares me
What do I do?

Thursday, 13th June 2013 - Stop Laughing and Understand

I had to sit back and hear someone laughing at someone with Mental Health condition because they didn't understand, they won't ever understand, but no respect. I hung my head in shame that someone could do this to another human, I know it happens, but, this is the sort of thing that needs to stop, I felt like turning around and saying you don't realise that I take tablets do you? and see what they say :-

Stop laughing at what is going on
You don't understand
Everything to you is so funny
Even more so when you don't understand
And when you know it is to do with Mental Health

She took tablets
So do I, I just haven't told you
For the same reason
I am sat here telling everyone not to laugh
Just because you don't understand

You may be the sort of person who may never understand
Good for you
You will never go through what we go through
But just remember that laughing can be
A sign of disrespect for that person

Did you ever think about asking them
How they were?
If they were alright??
No instead you just sit there now and laugh
Laugh at the situation they got themselves in

Did you ever think they were being controlled
By something beyond their control
By someone else
That is where I have been in the past
Now I am free

I am just not free enough to be able to tell you
Tell you what has happened
Because, now I know what will happen
I can't because it will all be a joke
You won't believe me because you are not adult enough

Adults will sit and listen
They don't sit and laugh
They have respect for those around them
Some will understand
Some will help you by talking

You have just belittled
What I have got
I wouldn't want you to go through
What we are going through for anything
Not to have to rely on tablets to keep you going
Or to keep you working.

I want to talk about this
But, it seems like that it could be the worst thing possible
Because some will only see it as a laugh
As I have said one day you will understand

And suddenly realise what we are going through

Thursday, 13th June 2013 - I Want You to Stop & Think Before You Speak

I saw a opening this week, but as you can see the door got slammed again!! I am not giving up :-

Help Me understand
Understand why you can't hear me
Why you want to shut me out
Not just shutting but slamming the door
A big thick wooden door

This week I thought I saw the hole
The hole in which the door closed
But after today,
It slammed again
Because you laughed

You are so scared, so afraid
Of what you don't know
So you talk about it as if it was a joke
You know there is something wrong
But, you can't bring yourself to ask

Would you like me to laugh at you
If I didn't understand
No, I didn't think you would
The anger in me is at boiling point
I am standing on my soapbox

You know that person
If you respect them you ask them
You don't just laugh
You try to understand what they are going through
There are times we don't understand

Try
That is all I ask
Try to understand
Try to talk about what is going on
Not to shun me

I get low like today
I feel ashamed when I cry
Cry at work
Cry in front of all those people
Because I can't stop

I want to stop this hurting
I want to laugh again
I want to go out again
I want to be able to joke again
I want to be able to smile not just paint one on.

I want you to stop and think
Perhaps ask that person before you laugh at them
Help yourself to understand what they are going through

Thursday, 13th June 2013 - Together We Will Stand United

The only way we are going to do this is to stand together :-

We have to start it
But in order to start it
We have to be united
Stand together
Help each other

We need to stand united
Not only to beat our Mental Health problems
But to break down
The doors of silence

The walls that have been up for so long
The doors that have started to open
If we push it
United we will stand

We can shout and cry
Cry tears of joy
Because finally someone has heard us
But it will only happen if we take a stand

I want to take each wall down
Brick by brick
Word by word
Shout after shout

We will be heard
And one day we will be understood
Come and stand by me
Straight and tall, let your voice be heard

For every brick taken
Another word is understood
One more written
To getting our voices heard

For our Minds to be understood
We are all complex
In many different ways
With time we will understand

Stand united
We won't fall
We can only get stronger
With that speech we will get better

Stand together
Shout loud enough
And destroy those walls
We will be heard stood United

Thursday, 13th June 2013 - I Want You to Stop & Think Before You Speak

I saw a opening this week, but as you can see the door got slammed again!! I am not giving up :-

Help Me understand
Understand why you can't hear me
Why you want to shut me out
Not just shutting but slamming the door
A big thick wooden door

This week I thought I saw the hole
The hole in which the door closed
But after today,
It slammed again
Because you laughed

You are so scared, so afraid
Of what you don't know
So you talk about it as if it was a joke
You know there is something wrong
But, you can't bring yourself to ask

Would you like me to laugh at you
If I didn't understand
No, I didn't think you would
The anger in me is at boiling point
I am standing on my soapbox

You know that person
If you respect them you ask them
You don't just laugh
You try to understand what they are going through
There are times we don't understand

Try
That is all I ask
Try to understand
Try to talk about what is going on
Not to shun me

I get low like today
I feel ashamed when I cry
Cry at work
Cry in front of all those people
Because I can't stop

I want to stop this hurting
I want to laugh again
I want to go out again
I want to be able to joke again
I want to be able to smile not just paint one on.

I want you to stop and think
Perhaps ask that person before you laugh at them
Help yourself to understand what they are going through

Thursday, 13th June 2013 - Together We Will Stand United

The only way we are going to do this is to stand together :-

We have to start it
But in order to start it
We have to be united
Stand together
Help each other

We need to stand united
Not only to beat our Mental Health problems
But to break down
The doors of silence

The walls that have been up for so long
The doors that have started to open
If we push it
United we will stand

We can shout and cry
Cry tears of joy
Because finally someone has heard us
But it will only happen if we take a stand

I want to take each wall down
Brick by brick
Word by word
Shout after shout

We will be heard
And one day we will be understood
Come and stand by me
Straight and tall, let your voice be heard

For every brick taken
Another word is understood
One more written
To getting our voices heard

For our Minds to be understood
We are all complex
In many different ways
With time we will understand

Stand united
We won't fall
We can only get stronger
With that speech we will get better

Stand together
Shout loud enough
And destroy those walls
We will be heard stood United

Thursday, 13th June 2013 - Night Night

Well, we have come to that time of day, with my last post to you all, Night Night each one of you and peace to you all have a good night's sleep so I can talk to you tomorrow.

I have stood a many a morn
Looking out my bathroom window
Seeing the sun fill the sky
And the glory of the colours that surround

Tonight I stood there once more
To see the splendour over again
Except it wasn't the rising of the sun
It was the setting with fantastic gold

The colours reached across the sky
Across the landscape that rolled anigh
I saw the reaching of the clouds
As they blanketed the sky thoroughly

As I sit on my own tonight
I hear nothing around
I can't even hear the birds
Because they all said good night

The peace and tranquility
That surrounds the house
Along with the many greens that cover the fields
And the greens in the trees

The birds fly by to their nests
The babies they have left
The ones that they are about to feed
As they say night night to me

I will say alas
They are right as the sky turns dark
But, I will still be here when the morning imparts

Good evening to you all and one good night

Friday, 14th June 2013 - My Name is..... And I Stand Up

This is what you would call very heavy, but, unless I say and keep quiet then I am guilty of keeping silent like everyone who doesn't say so here goes and I am sorry if it is heavy and rather strong for you :-

Have you heard my voice?

Do you see my tears?

Have you watched my footsteps?

I didn't think so because you are still deaf, you are still blind, you still don't look around you at what is happening.

Let me spell this out to help you understand and it is the bravest thing I have ever done, some will say, but for me I want to tell you what this is like.

My story starts here I have moved around so much in my lifetime never settling down anywhere most of all now in my marriages and with men, jobs and homes now.

Twenty years ago was the first time I knew that I had depression, since then I have discovered that I have been in and out of it. I HAVE DEPRESSION NOW, I wanted to shout that to tell you and others I am not scared.

Over the twenty years of depression, I have tried to take my life twice, saved by friend and mum once and then again by the fire service with a fire in my building(not my room), I want to tell you that I wish it had happened, but, I am happy to tell you that I am glad it did not, otherwise, I wouldn't be here to tell my story today, that I wouldn't have the support of the strongest most beautiful and amazing man I know.

I have been in and out of three abusive marriages filled with controlling people, since August last year, this is the first period in my life I have not had someone saying don't do that, I can't do that, you need to do this, when are you coming home, I have had a period of my phoning not ringing constantly or texts coming through or blame being given to me.

I have also had 5 dvt's which this has attributed to my depression of not wanting to do the things I used to do and medically not being able to fly where I want to fly, but, now I have a man I want to do that travelling with I can't do it, but we know we will find a way.

Enough of me and my life, I have had good parts to it and it started in August when I found someone else. Someone who cared. Little did I know that I was going back down again until the end of it, what I didn't realise was that I have never really come out of my depression just sat and suppressed it until I found someone new, someone who understood.

In October, my new man broke down and realised he was breaking down, I supported him through all the months once again suppressing until he was strong enough to help me through it all.

Now I want to stand with others and tell my story. This is my voice I am working very hard to get through this on my own, but know I need help by pulling on my strengths, my writing and feelings.

Each day I have written how strong to be, pick up each piece and help yourself get stronger. That picture or collage of mine is starting to come together, looking at it I can shine from it, I can say that was me and it has helped to get where I am.

I wouldn't have been able to do this without the help of the people around me, little do they know it but the people in work, even though they know nothing about me, building my confidence back up bit by bit. I wish I could just help them understand me and what is different.

I want to help them understand what is happening, I want you to stand with me to help me help others to help others to help others. There is too much ignorance, too much avoidance too much silence and too much blindness of what goes on with mental health.

If we all hold hands, stand together united as a family and speak about it we will get through this, we will be able to help the stigma for Mental Health.

My name is Susan Bell aka Heartily Mindful, I have been guilty of being silent for far too long and now I am crying, crying out my story to stand strong with others because I no longer feel ashamed about suffering from depression no matter what, I will stand up for and alongside of people with Mental Health I will give support and write, posting wherever I can to be heard so that one day there will be a clearer understanding and support for me with those with Mental Health.

I am Susan Bell, I am not my illness I have a Mental Health condition called Depression.

Please stand with me to help lift the stigma.

Thank you for listening and hearing what I have said.

Friday, 14th June 2013 - Take the Courage

Courage
That is all it takes
One word to stand alone
But it also takes
Many of us to stand together

Take the Courage
To stand up and be heard
Stand up in the hole
Where you have taken out those bricks

I feel there are still so many of us who want to shout about this, but, it doesn't matter if you don't stand with those of us who do and help to lift the Mental Health Stigma:-

Hold onto the courage
So that you can help others
To turn their lives around
To let them tell their story
So that we can help lift the barriers

I have the courage
I have told my story can you
Be brave
Hold on to what you have
Listen to those around you

Hear what they have to say
Take the courage to stand up for it
Stand up for what is right
To help Mental Health become noisy
Not just a dreaded silence

I am still there
I told my story to come out of it
Hear what I have to say
And you never know how much it will help you
Help you and your Mental Health

Friday, 14th June 2013 - History Swept Away

My day and history have helped me today as I packed to move home, made jewellery and wrote my story.

I tripped the light fandango today
I walked a thousand miles
I drove to somewhere new
I stood and shouted out my name
I supported my Mentally ill Partner

What have I done you ask
What did I do
Where did I go
Why did I dance and walk
Because I picked up a piece of my picture

I held a piece of glass in my hand
Cut my hand and bled
Then that piece of glass turned to a piece
Piece of picture of my past
A piece which I can now place on the canvas

I stuck the piece where I wanted it to go
Not where It was
Or where it is supposed to go
It got stuck in a place where it needed to go
Where I could get past it

One was I told my story
That was enough to get past
The next I threw out clothes
I looked at them saying they weren't me
And the relief of doing all this

The pieces that have given me the strength
The strength to be able to help someone
Someone else who needs me
Needed my support
Today was the day that scared me

Now I can start to look forward
to get past everything
Start to blow away the cobwebs
The ones that have been there for too long
The old ones that don't seem to move

I have promised myself they will this time
So I can help others
I can write what I need to
To help others
We will all make it

Saturday, 15th June 2013 - I Stand Up for Men's Mental Health

As some of you will know it is Men's Mental Health Week this week. I thought I would give you a brief piece on my other half's Mental breakdown. I am trying to resound what is being said that we have to realise that all of us male or female can have a Mental Health problem at anytime in our lifetime, we should all be helping each other whomever we are stop the silence not be ashamed of what we have got or who we are:-

How many men do you know that have walked a mile, when all they needed to do was walk one foot?

Would you want to walk in every man's footsteps?

Have you spoken to a crying man recently?

I have. I have for the past 10 months I have sat and watched a grown man cry, someone who everyone knew as a hearty, bubbly person laughing all the time not crying at anytime or looking sad, thinking hard about things that have happened in the years that have passed him by.

It took two months of discussion with myself and practitioners to realise that he was suffering from depression and breaking down mentally. To him he felt he was being weak in realising or owning up to this, but, as you and I know this was the first step.

The first step towards getting better and strength, because he could finally make himself well again and he is now on the mend.

All I can say is that I have been with him right from the beginning, to be able to see how he has grown from strength to strength. His reasons for his Mental breakdown were all sorts of reasons
and he needed to ask for help, but, never give in.

He found himself someone new to love, me, he worked hard and was working hard, his started to become ill in himself, which is where I started to see the signs, he had a bad back which was the last thing that took him, it took a month after that to suddenly realise I was right and so was the doctor who had been seeing him for his back. I would also like to add to this that he was caring for his mum.

He slowly went into the stupor we all do with depression of not wanting to do anything except ask for help with the counselling and to sit and cry with me. This is no weakness in fact I see at a strength even though he couldn't tell me what it was he wanted to talk about, I stood by him, held him and encouraged him that crying is helping him. Helping him to keep together as he would say to me that if it wasn't for me...I don't like to think about that.

As I recovered from my fifth DVT, I helped him to look after his mum, helping him to get better whilst trying to work, this isn't sympathy for me I want, it is a resounding round of applause for him as we both looked after each other through our illnesses, mine seen and his unseen which was the difference. Me, female and him male with an unseen illness which is the other difference.

If I was to say that his recovery was easy and quick I would be lying, because at times it has been very hard and a struggle, but, still I love him for having the strength to get through his problems, to place a piece of his history picture together along the way so that one day he can look back and smile to say it has got him to a stronger person and he got past it all.

There is nothing wrong with a man having depression, you have to encourage to cry, to help him realise that he has what he has and you can see him past the depression or mental health illness, perhaps if there was more realisation that a man can have this they may go to the doctors or be more help in a male orientated company for Mental Health for all the staff.

For any man reading this who thinks they may have depression reach out and tell someone, it is not a weakness to be seen admitting it, most of us at one time in our lives suffer from a mental health illness, some do not admit it and not ask for help others do like me.

I hold my hand up and out to any man who does admit it, it doesn't mean you have to stop work, just ask for help, there is nothing wrong with it in fact it is right.

I am so proud and even cry at the fact I have a very strong man now, someone I look up to even more than before, I would say that I supported him through it, but, he has done most of the work and it has been hard work. He now encourages me and supports me through my depression as he knows what to expect.

Please if you are a man it doesn't matter what level of Mental Health you have stand up and ask for help there is no shame, you deserve as much help as we do. Ask your doctor, friends, even Mind or Rethink or any other Mental Health Organisation for help.

I am not going to name, names as that again is unfair. I stand up and salute you, I am proud of what you have done and how strong you have become for admitting to what you thought was your weakness, I am so proud that we have gone through this to make our relationship go from strength to strength and realise that you are not frightened to show your emotions or feelings to me and knowing you can talk to me about anything. Thank you that you have let me share and support you through this. I love you very much always!

Sunday, 16th June 2013 - Hand in Hand Stop the Silence (Not a poem)

Wow, that hurt and the tears did roll inside, but, now is time for me to tell this joint story as I told the separate ones of how me and my partner stood side by side to hear each other and understand one another through our depression. Please read our story after hearing our solo ones:-

Have you understood what I said?

Have you listened to what I said?

Do you know where I am?

I can answer yes to all of those, because I have been here before. There are others who haven't and don't understand what is going on.

There is so much silence everywhere about Mental Health that is so deafening!!

I think I first started my depression in my twenties, my first husband understood, but didn't really. My second well there is no such thing it is all in their minds, so I hid mine from him, I was on painkillers that were also antidepressants for my leg ulcers easy to do. My third husband understood because he had been through it before, but, didn't really want to sit and listen or hear me, just keep going to the counsellor or the doctor you will be ok.

So how do I know that my partner is hearing me now?

How do I know he understands?

Because he had a mental breakdown, two months after we got together, for the reason he had someone understanding standing by him and could hear what he was saying before he could. He wanted to carry on saying that it was just his back when myself and his doctor knew that he was going through depression and needed help.

I was starting to hold mine back at this time as well, I held him as he would cry, I said that he could talk, but, he told me that he didn't know how, I felt hopeless and useless especially as I could feel myself slipping down into my depression again very slowly knowing I had to stay strong for him and his mum with the new family who were starting to get to know me. When I asked what use was I then, he would tell me the fact I was there and I could understand with hearing what he was saying without saying it.

I was standing by my man, I felt proud on top that I was supporting him, but, the tears came underneath, this is a tough job for any partner to do, especially if you know where you are going.
Most of his friends didn't understand how to accept or to talk to him, I would probably say neither did his family.

At this time I had just got my 5th DVT in my left leg up and down to hospital, back and forth, you could probably say this was a trigger to mine, but, it started before that. I did go back to work for a couple of days driving over a hundred miles a day, the doctors signed me to work from home, which I did, so when I was working from home I was helping with his ill mum and my partner as he slept most of the day from painkillers for his back.

I don't think that he knew what a road this was going to take him down until he looks back today and realises how far he has gone or come if you want to see it like that. I was there to hold him with the tears and when he got angry, I am pleased(not the right word) to have been there that it was me with him not someone else.

He started on antidepressants after much persuasion, which helped, they took their time in starting as they do, at this time I moved to a work that was closer to home easier for me and if needed at home I could get there. Everything started to look up as the tablets and counselling started to help things. I was there when he came out of them, when he needed to just cry and not talk.

This was the time when I started to want to be more on my own and not around people, because they couldn't understand me and how I was acting, it was one Sunday afternoon he had come up to the bedroom after I had spent some time up there and I just cried, I told him that I was in a depression, he held me and said I thought that you were, you have been changing for so long, just little things time to get some help.

I plodded on for a couple of more weeks and it was getting worse I would have bad sleepless nights, crying a lot, getting angry, I had suppressed my feelings for so long, until he got strong enough to be able to support me, I don't want sympathy for this as I shouldn't have done it because it made things worth as it had in the past. By now my partner was getting upset with this because I needed to do something about it, I did that night, I went for a drive and then to my home. Everything was alright.

The next day I called the doctors, my doctor helped me by saying that I needed to see a counsellor to start with and if I needed more help, so I had finally reached out for help, but, the bad days had got closer and closer together, my partner held me with the tears and heard me when I needed to talk, which was like my writing a rambling mess!

Now I am on tablets to help me, this helps with my concentration at work, but, I still have not said out loud at work what has happened, the silence there is deafening and hard to accept, I bring all my low moods home I wish that the silence would stop, I want my real smile not a painted one.

This is why I am writing because I want there to be someone to be able to talk to at work if I need it. I want my friends who don't understand to be able to understand. I want the whole World to hear how two completely different conditions of Mental Health have worked together and stand together to support each other.

I want to tell our stories so the stigma stops. It is not only outside of your own partnership to understand but inside too, hearing what the other has to say instead of thinking they are in a low mood everyday ask them if they are really alright if there is something they need to talk about, show them that you care, if you love each other don't just walk away, you will fight together, I know you say it is easy enough for me to say, it hasn't we haven't been together a year yet.
I want the World to understand that Mental Health is not a disease it is an illness that can be helped if we all stand together to help it and each other!!

Thank you for listening to me!! Now I want you to stand with me to lift the stigma, we will get there with each person that understands.

We both stand together hand in hand now to support Mental Health and to stop the silence on every level!!

Sunday, 16th June 2013 - Silence, I Want To Explain

I want you to hear what I am saying, what I want to say, I am not sure how far this is going, I want it to reach those around the world who don't understand as this is what I have to say:-

Silence is around me as I sit here trying to listen
But it is too deafening
The dumbness I am forced to play
Because you just don't understand
You can't hear what I say

If only you took the time
To sit with me a while
To understand what is happening to me
I don't have to tell you all of it
Just enough for you to hear me

Come and sit down
Listen to my words
I have days where I can be happy
Then no sooner said than done my mood can be gone
The lowness that I hate

That lowness is like a large heavy black cloud
One that hovers around my head
And what is going on inside is so confusing
Frustrating even, because I can't understand
Letting you know how I can get helps me

It will stop you from telling silly things
Like "Snap out of it", "Stop being so moody"
When all it is like is a switch turned off in my head
I stand here on my own
When really all I want to do is say something for you to hear me

There is a lot more to all of this
But, for the time being as long as you understand the basics
That is all our silence needs to stop
So that at least you can stop treating me like a child with a tantrum
Because I'm not, I have issues that I can't get past at the moment

The emptiness and numbness
Is another thing, something deeper inside
The thought of meeting with people each and every day
Some old some new
That's what is also an issue

What I can't tell you about is the sickness deep inside
The sicky, tired feeling of wanting to do nothing
This is all the pain from my past
Little by little I pick up each piece
That piece will then slot into where I want it to go

As I do this you will see a newer me
My moods will start to lift
But, for the time being I need help to take me away from these
As I sit here typing this to you
I am helping myself

As I help myself I am hopefully helping others
I no longer want this gap between you and me
A long lost silence because we can't talk
I want it to be broken down to you understanding
Understanding how I am feeling

I want to break this silence
To be able to help you understand
To listen to what we both say
To hear what is around me not just the deafening silence
One day you will hear me and the silence will be gone

Until then your silence to you is golden
Mine is deafening
All I ask is you try to understand what I write
Perhaps you may reach out to me
But, mainly stop me from hearing the silence

Sunday, 16th June 2013 - Are Silence & Darkness Your Old Friends?

I am at the moment finding the sound of silence deafening and the darkness my dear old friend blinding, why can I find nobody that will hear me to talk to them and I keep getting doors slammed in my face:-

Hello darkness, my old friend
I've come to talk with you again
The sound of what I can hear around me
Is nothing
Only the thoughts running around my head

When I listened to the thoughts
I wanted to tell them that they were so wrong
That all I could hear was silence
I could see people talking
But, the silence grew stronger

I have been here before
My friend I just want some help from you
There is too much around me
I just need to sit here quietly and calmly
I know to many that doesn't make sense

What I need is to understand how
And why this has happened again
Why I am back here with you again
I need to plan what I need to do
But, I am too confused, frustrated at what is going on

If I could just ask someone to help me
There is no-one around me to understand
I want to shout
But my voice only comes out as a whisper
I can't feel anything inside myself except the pain of what has started this

If only there was someone to ask for help
If I can't understand how can anybody else
I just want the doors to stop closing
I want someone to ask me how I am
The silence has to stop it hurts both inside and out

Monday, 17th June 2013 - What am I?

This is a question I keep asking, one that everybody with a mental health illness asks:-

Who am I?
What am I?
Am I an individual?
Am I independent?
Or does my illness describe me?

Where do I come from?
Where do I belong?
How long will I last?
Where am I going next?
Will this ever end?

What is inside?
Can I change?
How do I do it?
What do I do next?
Where can I go?

I am a human being
With a deep soul
An illness that is a darkness inside
The illness is not me
I am have this illness

My illness is depression
I ask for help as the tears roll down
And the darkness rises up to greet me
It greets me when it likes
With this all people see is my depression

I am a person underneath
I am not hiding from all of this
I want the silence to stop
The doors to stop slamming
Because my ears are ringing and hurting

I am trying to tame
If not get rid of the darkness in the deep
The darkness that I have had to hide from
For so long, too long
I want to speak out

It is time to make a stand
With as many people as possible
Saying who they feel
How depression or Mental Health makes them feel

I want stigma lifted from all over the world

Tuesday, 18th June 2013 - The Angel That Saved Me For A Reason

I want you to see how I have been feeling, believing in an Angel isn't always a religious belief:-

As I sit here in my silent solitude
I can feel something soft
That isn't the cloud that is covering my mind
It is the softness of the feathers
The feathers of an Angel

I have had an Angel with me
For as long as I can remember
One that has saved me twice
Or even more before
From the darkness that I feel inside

I may not know who they are
But I was given over 7 years ago
A third chance to walk this earth
To be able to say what I need to say
Even from behind closed doors

That Angel taught me a good lesson
The lesson is very well learnt
I will never do it again
I may think it
But it is enough I have people who care

I am here on Earth to spread one message
It isn't religious before you ask
It is to speak out
To stop silence, wherever you maybe
It may only be writing, that is my speech

I don't speak
I write
About the one thing I can understand
Because it is deep inside of me at the moment
It isn't going to stay

If I had the help twenty years ago
That I have now
If I hadn't hung my head in shame
If I hadn't done this, If I hadn't done that
But that was then this is now

I am not ashamed I have a Mental Health Illness
I will stand silently by or behind closed doors
I will tell the World what they need to
I will shout it from the rooftops
I want you to understand that this is an illness!!

Tuesday, 18th June 2013 - I Have a Mental Illness

I want people to understand what having a Mental Illness can do to someone, and how it can change them, but this doesn't meant they are the illness they just have the illness, listen to what I have to say below:-

There is one last thing I have to say
Don't be ashamed of who you are
Nor what you have
You have a Mental Illness
You are NOT that Mental Illness

With what I have seen and heard
The laughing
The sniggering
and people being rude
It is the not understanding what Mental Illness is

It is not funny
Or polite to poke fun at people
We are who we are
If you don't want to understand
Fine, don't and respect us

If you want to understand
Ask us,
We are more than happy to explain
It is not an easy thing to do
Live in a society who think we are monsters

A society
Where everybody thinks they are "Normal"
One day it may happen to you
Never ever say never
I know manager who have said that and wish they hadn't

Managers who now hang their heads in shame
Who wish that they could have helped that one person
The one person who could have been you
Cry out for help
Someone to talk to and a little encouragement

This goes for friends too
The ones who pushed you away
The ones who won't recognise they have a problem
Because they think it is weak to do this
I hate to tell you, you are the weak one for not recognising it

I have been strong enough
Along with whoever is reading this
To realise it is time that we stopped hiding
Stopped the silence
Behind the closed doors of anywhere and everywhere

Please hear me when I say I have Depression
I have a past that haunts me
But, I know that I am going to be doing something about that
I am asking and seeking help
To be able to move on with my life and help others

The illness is not me, I have the Mental Health Illness

Tuesday, 18th June 2013 - Country nights

Yes, it has come to that time of day when it is time for my head to stop thinking and say good night, have a good sleep and I will be back tomorrow:-

As I drove home
I saw the ever changing the colours
The flowers and the trees
The beautiful birds and the bees
When I opened the window the fresh smell

I got to my room for one of my last nights
Opened my windows
I could smell the sweet scent of the flowers
I could even smell the rye fields
Which rolled in front of me with a bright yellow

I have just heard the sound of the Tawny Owl
This must mean only one thing
That night time is nigh over the woods
That Even song is just about to finish
As the mist lies over the fields

When you hear the beautiful twittering of the birds
The greyness of the blanket in the sky
Over the great vast expanse of the countryside
You know it is nearly time to say good night
The haze gets thicker and the darkness gets nearer

Now I must come to the end of writing
As my sleepy fingers have been thinking way too hard
The difficulty of darkness is it creeps over you in many ways
So good night all
Just for tonight, have a long and peaceful sleep

Wednesday, 19th June 2013 - Sitting in Solitude It Is Easier!!

Today has been one of those days when you wish you could start the week over and over:-

Why do I feel like a failure in everything I do
What is it with me
Why can I never do anything right
I deliver me as a stupid idiot
And that is what I become

I am so ashamed of myself
So upset I don't know where to begin
I might as well be at home
Where I am not going to pester anyone
Where everyone would be much happier

I don't want to be here anymore
I want to stop being a burden to everyone
Even those who think they understand
When they are too busy to even stop
I want them to stop making everything perfect

I want them to look at me
I want them to talk to me
I want them to see how I am feeling
To know what is deep inside
Why I am feeling like this

I want to stop the tears from falling
It is hurting my eyes
I feel so isolated
It hurts
I am trying to take a deep breath, but, can't only shallow

I feel so left out
pushed out
Not really included at all
No-one is bothered what is happening
I am just a failure as a human

He doesn't know how to deal with it
He kept all of his emotions and anger in
I let all of mine out especially when he keeps asking
I am just better off going home

Sitting on my bed in solitude

Thursday, 20th June 2013 - Stop The Silence & Hear The Shouting!!

I want you to listen to what I have to say, it may not be much, but, it is what made me write my piece from last night:-

I made one step forward
I talked
Talked to the one person who listened
He came looking for me
Perhaps he realised just what was going on

I was feeling at my lowest ebb last night
I was feeling desperate
I knew that I wouldn't do anything
But, I felt hopeless
As if there was nothing or nobody in my life that cared

I wanted to ask about me
Not to be talking about my partner and his garden all the time
I wanted my new family to ask about me
His stories are better than mine
Only because he has done everything better

I wanted my new family to see me
I wanted them to hear what I had to say
Nobody was bothered when I walked off
They thought I had gone in to do something else and left me
Until my partner found me

He found me crying
Because I so wanted to be heard
In both word and voice
Someone to find me interesting
To hear my story as well as his

When I talked he heard
He said that my stories are just as interesting
That he wanted to hear me
He wanted to know about me
So we talked until my tears stopped

Today had started badly
But the end was better
I walked in the garden gate
My partner was there to greet me
He held me and kissed me

I know now that I was heard
Last night is a painful desperate past
Full of hope and despair
Today, I took the first step to better me
I blocked out the people around me

I stopped trying to hear
Thinking that people were watching me
It was difficult
Tomorrow is going to get better
As I speak to another counsellor

The weekend is the end of the week
The time to refresh ourselves
Stop and think about the week that has gone
Freshen ourselves with friends and family
To be able to do lovely things

Come out from the darkness
Come into the light
Walk down the road
Find a friend and talk
It will help

The one thing I ask you
Is try to help someone understand
Help them to see you for you
And then understand the illness you have

Stop the silence and hear the shouting!

Thursday, 20th June 2013 - Stop This Silence!!!

I am not quite sure where to come from with this except I want to stop the stigma of mental health, my own depression and everyone around me:-

What I don't want to be known as
Moody
Emotional
Stressed
Attention seeking
Yet strong person

I'm not
I have an illness
One that if was to tell everyone
I would be shunned
I would be stereotyped, in fact I already have been

I don't want to be known as
Always quiet
Angry
Wanting to be on my own
Yet, smiling

Because I paint that smile on
Every day I mooch around
I have to get up to go to work
I paint on the smile
To help the sickness inside subsides

I want to tattoo it on my forehead
Like the tattoo on my back
I am depressed
I want the angel to keep her wings around me
So that I am safe as I shout about it

I know that won't happen
I will stay safe
But, I will have to get out
I have opened up to a lot of you
Now, it is time to start stepping up

I want to tell people
How it feels to be shut out of what is supposed to be normal
It isn't
At one time in our lives many of us will get an issue
Don't say it won't be me because it may be

I want you to understand the dark place you go to
How hard it is to come out
When there is nobody to understand
When there is no-one to help

Friday, 21st June 2013 - It is an Illness, I know Because I have it!!

I don't think I need to say too much to this piece except please read it :-

What do you want?

Where did you come from?

Why have you hurt me so much?

The answers to all these questions are depression. To be honest the first is that it wants to hide me in a corner and me to hide behind it

Twenty years ago I would have done that, ten years ago the same, five years ago the same again, six months ago NO! I will not let this happen to me all over again, I have had enough, I need to take a fight against what darkness and anger has arisen from inside of me over the years.

When I first had depression it was mild, but, still enough to try to take my own life, however if it wasn't for a very good friend who I made a pact with and kept I would never have been alive today, I pulled through it with determination as you do when you are younger hoping it will never rise again, but, it was just like a monster under the surface of my soul that would rear it's ugly head up and come up at anytime it wanted to.

I have always worked hard at trying to keep it down, but, one thing after another would lead me back to it's door and it would fully take over me, never really talking about it because I was ashamed of what I was ILL!

I was too young to understand, which didn't help, I learnt since my last big episode of depression that Mental Health is not shameful it is an illness, unfortunately one that has lain below the surface for far too long.

Big events in my life overtook me and they were major enough to me, which made my illness worse and the monster roar louder, even more so when there was someone close to you who said that depression is all in your head there is nothing wrong with you and it wasn't until I was taken off my painkillers(coincidentally anti-depressants) that I realised I had gone through depression as well.

What had made me struggle through life was the fact I kept hanging my head with shame and others who didn't understand what I couldn't explain to them or myself what was going on, now I am starting to understand a lot more, it has taken me a lot longer to think about as everything in my life, it has come with experience, my university of Life.

My understanding of it is I have to be the one to realise that the illness I have is real and as any illness I cannot get better until I ask for help or look for it. Once I had started on this road I thought to myself I am getting better, however even then I realised that I needed more help than just my supportive partner, doctor and once a month counsellor with my Fluoxetine, I need to talk more regularly and to help myself come out of this completely of manage it better.

I did that today and I sit here to tell you that it may have made things feel more real with the tears and opening up to another person, progressively it will help me.

One day the monster will subside or even vanish with any hope, but if we don't stand up to ask for change we will never get it.

We have to hold our hands up, not hang our heads in shame, we have to stand up and be counted as people with an illness not the illness being us.

I want everyone to understand My name is Susan Bell I have an illness called Depression I have had it for twenty years and I am just learning if I do not talk to others then where does Mental Health stand a chance.

Understand what is going on under your noses friends, it could happen to you, it could even be happening to you, do not close that door again to me the silence isn't golden it is deafening and deadly, find someone to help, who you need to help, someone who needs you to talk to it doesn't matter if you don't understand now, you won't unless you hear them or talk to them. IGNORANCE IS NOT BLISS and neither is Mental Health, neither is it silent anymore, you will know about it or at least I have died trying at the age of 100, not 22 or 35 years old because nobody understands.

I would just like to say hear someone with a mental illness before you decide not to understand!!

Saturday, 22nd June 2013 - Healing Time

We are often told "Time is a great healer" what they don't realise is yes, it maybe, however it all depends what crops up in our lives on top of what is trying to heal, what has happened to me is one thing after another until now, I can finally start to realise that I have to get myself better that things need the time to heal and the helping hand of someone else. So the next time you get told say yes with the hope that nothing else will happen:-

Time will be a healer
It will take time
Is all I hear
So I am listening

Time can cure
It can also leave pain
Past time has no feeling
It is just numb

I want to walk past time
I don't want it to stop
I know I have walked into a new time
One that will keep going

There will be a time that this time
Will be so different to last time
It won't be sad
It will only be happy

Why? You ask
Because I will have no reason
I will be able to look back
I will be able to see what has happened

I want to be able to touch the past
To be able to say
You were my present
Now you are my history and past

The part of my life that helped
Helped me to get to where I am now
I will be able to say thank you

Thank you for what I have got now

Saturday, 22nd June 2013 - Wake Up, Smell the Coffee

I remember what happened and I thought that I was alright:-

The question is do you remember?

Do you remember when it first started?

How it first started?

Why it first started?

I remember, I was 22 years old when depression was such a private thing that even my parents were embarrassed to realise when I first started. They never realised that I had any kind of depression until I tried to kill myself.

If you read my blog during the week, I was saved by an angel that day for the reason of sitting here and telling you what you could be missing and what you are missing. Even though it is going through my mind about how low and hopeless I feel, I will never do it, because I am lucky enough to have an Angel standing by me to support me, one tattooed on my right shoulder.

I have been fortunate over the years to be able to paint the smile on, put a mask on of all laughs and smiles, but, now I cannot do it. The mask has hurt too much, caused too much pain, too many tears behind closed doors and in the silence that should never have happened

I want those who shut us out to realise what and why we feel the way we feel and that this is our illness. We just want to be able to talk about it as if we had chicken pox, hay fever or even flu! This will never work until we say something about what has happened to us.

I want there to be a network or someone within the workplace who is trained to help hear what we are saying for just a few minutes, we want to be accepted in the workplace as people who have RSI or back problems. I want contractors to be able to call a counselling line outside of work not just permanent staff so they can receive help as well instead of sitting in silence when needing help, especially as there are so many of us around in companies.

We have all hidden behind masks and we still do even more so at work which hurts the most. These are the people we trust to help us with our work each day, pay our wages each month or week, yet we cannot trust them with the one thing we so desperately need to say something about, for them to understand that we can work with our Mental Health illness if we had someone else to help us.

I have problems with telling them because of losing my contract, I have so many times wanted to go to my manager and tell her that I am really applying for a four day week because I need the fifth to help me deal or get my self better from my depression, but, like a lot of you am worried that because it is a stressful job she will think that I am not capable of doing my work. Me depression as nothing to with work, yet it affects my work in a few ways only with the people not the work or stress.

If only the managers would hear what we have to say because one day it may be them, one day they could fall ill as we have and wished they that they had just one person they could have spoken to. By then it is too late or could it be? that is the question for the manager.

Would they know what it is like to feel agitated, nervous even sick in the morning to walk in an office even the best contract you have ever been on knowing that you are not treated the same as a permanent member of staff to talk to that someone or network of someone in the office.

That you have a low mood during the day that triggers your quietness, when if you had spoken when you needed it. That you are angry by the time you get home at the person you love so much and supports you throughout your illness.

I want to hear managers ask if I am alright and really ask are you alright not just at that moment or if I had a good evening.

All I ask for is understanding of what I have, that I no longer have to hide from you or my colleagues, that I can stand and be heard and treated normally. That my partner can go to an interview and his mental state is not counted against him. I don't want to be counted as a statistic within a firm because they say that mental health is a disability it isn't we just have problems from the past we are working to get past.

I am working to be a stronger person, I took one step forward yesterday, I asked for extra help, my illness has never hit me for so long before, but, I realise it is because I am trying to work it from a different angle of learning to live and work with it, I am willing to sacrifice a little bit of money just so I can get my life back on track and I will day be able to give all those in my past a massive thank you.

I am Susan Bell, I have Depression and I stand for lifting Mental Health Stigmatism in the workplace and to all those who don't understand.

Thank you for reading this piece today.

Sunday, 23 June 2013 - Weather it

I have felt the rain falling on my clipped wings
I have felt the wind chill my heart with bars
I have felt the sun burning on my white back
as my legs walk down a long windy road
towards the cross roads I finally reached

My head had to make a decision
do I stay or do I go
I knew what I had to and I did it
I left
I turned to the left and I still found the sun on my back

The tears still kept on flowing
I couldn't find the direction
I looked straight ahead and knew it wasn't right
I looked to the right, the brick wall had fallen
The bars had come off

My head had made the decision
My clipped wings had become unfurled
My heart began to beat again
Most of all My face was in the sun I was walking towards it
A smile on my face

I am feeling free again
The sun on my face, my wings and my heart
Nothing will ever do that to me again
I am me, me is me
I am finally relaxing to being free again
I feel proud of being that beautiful and amazing person in the sun

I AM FREE!!

Monday, 24th June 2013 - Quiet?!!

I have heard the silence which is truly deafening, the silence of no maddening thoughts, which usually means there is something starting up, perhaps after my really low week someone is giving me a break? :-

I can hear quiet
I am not sure if this is peace
Or the lull before the storm
And soon the thoughts will go running through

I sat at work today and thought
Nothing was working
I could hear nothing
I have had these feelings before though

I want to walk somewhere
Sit down and let my head go
I have been so wrapped up in things
I need to let it all go

Perhaps, tonight I will
Sit here and think about what is next
What step is next in my life
The thought of moving is shaking me

I have packed the boxes
Well nearly
And now it is time to move them out
I only have until the end of the week

After that I move in somewhere else
Somewhere exciting and new
I can make new friends
And meet with the old ones

Then the next step is me
Taking care of me finally
Making sure
I get better for good

But, there is one thing
I will never forget what I have been through
So that I can help others
I want to help take the silence away.

Tuesday, 25th June 2013 - I Feel So, So, So Lonely!!

I sat looking blankly at my screen as I do every day and I stop not remembering what is happening, I do then and hear the crowd behind me and around me and I feel so blocked out of everything:-

I sat at work not for the first time
Feeling alone
Whilst the bustle went on around me
I could hear the laughter of others
As I sat looking at my screen
I felt helpless, because it wasn't the first time

It hasn't been a long time since I felt it either
I have sat at my desk crying before
Hoping that nobody could see me
And they don't
I get up and walk off nobody asks me either

I will sit there and listen
Wanting so much to join in
But, I can't
I don't really want to
All I can see is the darkness of the clouds

If only there was one person
One person to help me join in
But that would scare me
I don't know why
Because I can still hear the talking around me

Nothing is helping
Not even trying to listen
Nothing is happening
Except total silence in my head
And total voice loss from my mouth

If only I wasn't stuck in this never ending silence
This never ending wave of loneliness
I feel so hopeless
So low

I feel so, so, so lonely

Tuesday, 25th June 2013 - My Plateau

This is the chilly eerie feeling I have at the moment and it is making me sick to the stomach as I don't know what I can do:-

I have come to a plateau
One that I am not sure what is happening
It seems like a very dark place
Where I can't see anything around me
Except shadows

The place I have come to is very eerie
It makes me shudder
The silence echoes
All around me
And the cold makes me shiver

All I can see are people moving
But they seem like blobs
Talking at me not to me
They want to keep telling me what to do
Yet, I still don't want to do it

It hasn't come to my time yet
My time to realise
Realise what I am here for
Why I am here
If I am here for a reason

I just don't know
As I said it is a plateau
One where I can't see what to do
The next step hasn't come along yet
I haven't reached it

The feeling I get is of drowning
Water all around me
Not holding me up
Just letting me breath
Allowing me to live

I want the numbness to feel again
The darkness to be light
The eerie to be peaceful and serene
The realisation that I am alive

Time to be with friends again

Tuesday, 25th June 2013 - My Countryside

As most know who read my blog at this time of night it is time for me to say night night, but, first I like to give you a touch of my countryside drive :-

As I sit behind the wheel of my baby
With the four wheels spinning
Along the grey winding roads
The wind blowing through the windows
On a beautiful and sunny summers night

I can smell the freshly mown grass
Or the hay in the fields
The poppies populating the rapeseed fields
And the Wild garlic from the woodlands
As I drive

I know I am nearing home
With the beautiful colours of the fields
As they have changed from brown to green
Some from green to yellow
A beautiful bright yellow as the sun falls behind them

The stone cottages stand alone
With the stone clad walls
And the stony driveways with roads leading from them
As I get out of my car
I can hear the evening calls

From the sounds of the Wood Pigeon cooing
And the other birds twittering
I rush to the top of the cottage
I open the windows
Just in time to hear the last call of the Tawny Owl hoot.

Now I would like to say good night
As I quite often do at this time
With the drive home and the packing
I have had a time

Telling you where I am

Wednesday, 26th June 2013 - Night, Night Migraine

As you can see I have had rather and uneventful day with lying in bed with a Migraine:-

Shut out the noise
Close all the curtains
Hear nothing around
Just how I wanted it today

Pour me a water
Plump up the pillows
Silence the pretty little birds
Let the darkness cover me

This is where I want to be
With a pain in my head
And a sickness in my stomach
Sleeping quietly behind closed curtains

What I needed today
Has been done
I have a fuzzy head now
Which will hopefully make for a clear day tomorrow

Night night Migraine!!

Thursday, 27th June 2013 - My Angels Watching Over Me

As I have lain here in my bed again, all I could think about is what has helped to save me over the last few months, especially the last few weeks, soft downy pillows, the dark rooms and where I could lay down and get through what I have done realising how real all of this is, how ill I really am:-

I am enfolded by angels wings
As I sleep
I can feel the softness of the feathers
They have been keeping me safe
From the migraine I have had and the feelings inside

It feels just like a duvet covering over me
Like the pillows I need
To lay my head
And the silence I need to sleep
To close my ears with peace

This doesn't keep the thoughts away
It hasn't stopped the thoughts either
I was at a low ebb
As low as the night before
As low as the week before

I had an angel who is able to talk to me
One that can help me
One that will hold me even when things go wrong
I have an angel that is with me all the time
She sits on my left shoulder blade praying

A lot of people told me if you have one done
It has to mean something
It does because I know that one is walking with me all the time
I may not remember she is there
Her wings hold me tight

I have another,
One more I know about
He stands by my side and is human
Not an angel except in his support and heart
It is his arm that enfolds me

I have this one person and two angels
For no other reason I can think of than
I am meant to be here
If you think to yourself
Look around you

See if there is someone
It doesn't matter how
Whether it is online
Telephone, Email or face to face

Speak to them

There will be someone to help you to talk

Thursday, 27th June 2013 - A Strange Day For Me

This day is a strange day and one where my thoughts are possibly working overtime:-

One day the ice will stop forming
As will the snow stop falling
So will the rain stop pouring
And the clouds stop blowing
Leaving the sky beautifully clear

When the dusk falls to eve
And the birds sing away
All I can hear is silence
There is nobody to talk to
No-one in my head

As the evening changes
And the clouds uncover the night
The sky in it's deepest blue
Holds stars that shine brightly
With the moon holding the brightest light

All I can hear is a whisper
A whisper telling me that things will be alright
I have been saved for many a reason
There are several that I can see now

If I was to tell you all
You would ask what my last piece was about,
You should know that being ill like this is one thing
And one time you can change your mind

One is to be able to tell you how I write
The other is being saved for the man I love
And for him to love me as I have never been loved before
As I have never loved anyone

Those are but a few I can tell you the others you will have to wait and see

Friday, 28th June 2013 - Silence Amongst Friends & Work!!

I think this piece will speak for itself, I just want to say I hope those who are reading it are friends and work colleagues of sufferers, if so ease up and hear what they actually have to say to them, being lonely in a crowd is hard, hearing silence in the middle of loud noise is deafening and being in the dark with light all around is the hardest part of this illness, so don't laugh at what they have to say hear them and talk to them even if it is 'I am here for you to talk to, I may not have the answers' believe me, if I had this one person or group of persons at work I would probably find things easier:-

What are you doing at work?

Why are you working if you are ill?

Why can't you claim benefits?

You can't really be ill if you are at work?

Why do people think they know my illness better than me, when they actually don't understand at all?

First answer, because even though you think it is not helping it is by giving myself a routine and something to get up for in the mornings. The last answer probably helps with the next question too, but to clarify, it helps me to be able to keep a normal life as any, but, it would help if there was somebody I could talk to.

Third question, because I can work, I can't afford to and because it makes me feel better still being in the mainstream of working life, that I am still contributing to something.

Why can't I be ill and work, you wouldn't say that to someone who was a diabetic, someone who had a heart condition, if I had a cold or even if I had flu in fact for the last two you would be telling me to get back to work there is nothing wrong with me.

For the last answer there is no quick response, read on:-

I have depression and yes, this is an illness, not one that can be as easily bandied about my workplace or my friends with as much belief or so easily as say Diabetes or someone with asthma, you would say take an inhaler or insulin injection, make sure you eat some sugar. I go to work, for months before my application for a four day week, I have been working a five day or four and a half day week and found no trouble, over the first month whilst waiting to see if I got the permanent post, with the decision and answer that this post wasn't mine I decided to make an application for 4 days a week, since then that is what I have been working.

The taking out of working that one day has helped me to start to get thinking time, a day to help my partner and his mum, also some time over the weekend for myself as well, which I suppose would be a step forward a lot of you think, I am waiting for an answer from my Manager to see if I can up until the end of my contract do just 4 days.

Why have I just decided to do this? Because I wanted to be proactive instead of reactive, II wish my manager could read this to help my application. I don't want to end up having to take a huge chunk of time out, I have a contract with a good company which will give me a good standing in the future for a longer term if not permanent contract.

The other reason for doing this now and why haven't I done it before, because I have a partner who supports me for it not saying I can't do it, why should you go part-time, when I can't I am older, we can't do this, we can't do that, when if I had taken time off one day a week instead of a whole chunk of time, I may have got further and would have understanding, I am sat here writing this piece.
I am at the moment struggling with some friends who don't understand anything of the above, because they saw me on a good day, drinking they think I am alright. They never sat and talk to me in fact when I do they say yes, I know I have been there.

What I would really like to say is did you get sexually and physically abused?

Were you controlled to the state that you now don't trust people?

Were you watched so much because they wanted to know what you were doing every minute and you can't bare anyone watching you now thinking that it is still like that, when all they have done is hurt and damaged you.

I wouldn't say no, but, sit and listen to me not listen with a door in between, this is the same for work, everyone says they understand but, they don't, there is only one person that hears and can calm me down that is the only support I have for the past week he has heard me three times when I have been really low and a fourth, but the first three I was "So Low", for those who understand what I am saying, for those who want to I felt like I shouldn't be here. The fourth, my partner knew how to hit the spot by sending me a beautiful song, which even though I still felt low I was there with it and he calmed me down.

You see, just because I work, because, I have a good day, because I smile, because I look normal, because I am extremely low, I am ill, there are times when I think there is something wrong, but, the fact that the doctor has given me Fluoxetine(also known as Prozac) demonstrates that I am ill, because you can't cheat the doctor ever, they have given me numbers for counsellors. I see a counsellor at the moment once a month.

My illness differs from person to person, so friends do not compare mine to my partners, we have both had it for different reasons, I stood by him until he was strong enough to support me, I was being selfish, it seems to others who think I should not be doing this and have asked if he is alright, what they do not realise is he is trying to help me, he has been busy with trying to get the garden done, going out with friends, helping me with making jewellery (trying to keep me in one of the things I enjoy) just I did with him when he was ill, taking him out for photography with a trip to Slimbridge, and flying birds which we both enjoyed I might add.

So what I would like to add is open up your doors and hear what we both have to day not just the first part and then close it again.

Hear what I have to say to you, please, I am ill I have depression and I have never felt so low because I thought my friends were understanding me and have heard me. I feel sick to my stomach and could cry a whole of sea of tears from inside and out, if you don't believe me ask the person who has sat watching me for the past couple of months getting worse.

I want employers, colleagues and friends to hear me that shutting the door to what you don't understand is not the answer to hiding it, it is just the avoidance of the issue that is all around you. Just because, I am not pale, I am not throwing up, I'm not needing an inhaler, nor an injection, I just need someone to talk to, if there was one person I could trust to talk to not to laugh at me or to gossip around or just to give me five minutes to let me cry I would make up whatever time it would take.

All the above could be you at anytime for any reason in your life, mine is my past trying to get on with my future and helping others with theirs.

My tears are now inside for you for not understanding, talk to me, ask me what is truly going on, read all my blog and see how far I have truly gone, I have had everything I needed around me to do what I have felt like doing, but, I have stopped because one person especially if not a few more have held their hands out to me and asked how I AM not, just how are you!

All I can say is I take the Courage to say my name is Susan Bell, I am 42 years old and I suffer from depression. I work for a living as well as writing this blog telling my feelings daily expressing how I feel from deep inside, I also make and sell jewellery for a living and write books.

All I want you to do is hear what I have to say and not stand in silence anymore with the loneliness I have stood in a crowd.

Thank you for reading!!

Friday, 28th June 2013 - The Stronger Person I Want To Be!!!

I have wanted to feel like this for a bit, but, I am still unsure if this is the beginning or the end or just the start of recovery. I moved my own home today with a little help, but, this is a new step on my never ending journey to pursuit of being a better person:-

Where does it start
When does it end
Where is the middle
Of anyone's time
Time that we need to sit back and think

What does it matter
Who does care
Only the people who can see you
See through you to you centre
Perish that thought

Anyone who can see through me
Are welcome
They can try
It won't be easy seeing through
What I see as a tangled up mess inside

The pain and hurt
Then more comes along to hit me
Hit me where it hurts even more
Enrages me until the end
Soon enough I feel the tap on the shoulder

The tap that reminds me
That I am not alone
The one thing that is sure to remind me
That I have someone to help me
Someone to talk to

No, it isn't easy for my angel to do that
I don't care if you believe
One day I will be let down to Earth
With or without a bump
She will let me go

I will have another on my shoulder
Take a look
You will see this one cannot go anywhere
I don't want her to
There is also a man who helps me

This man helps to unravel my pain
He helps my pain to go away
It is when I am alone I feel it most
I know I have to be on my own
To be able to work through this pain

I have worked through a little
And I have more to work out
Slowly, slowly I pick up the pieces
To be able to become that stronger person
The one my Angels want me to be

The stronger person I want to be!!

Friday 28th June 2013 - My strength

I have been sitting and thinking too much today I think :-

I want to be
I will be
The person
That I want to be

I will be stronger than you want
Stronger than I feel
Stronger than I have ever been
Before

What you see before you
Is not what I really am
There will be a strength rise up
So that I can be who I want to be

When you see me one day
I won't recognise
I will strong, beautiful and amazing
There will come a time

I will rise up from the ashes I am in now
The ashes will have cooled
They will have scattered
Scattered back to where they came from

I will start one day
You will then find me
Not hiding under the bushes
But out in the open

I can then say
I did this my way
With some help
I took my strength and put it inside of me

Saturday, 29th June 2013 - Simply and Plainly My Illness

I wanted to tell you where everything started and how, but, if you read through, things through my history have just tripped me up and brought me here today, take a look:-

Where did it all come from?

How did it all start?

I don't know is the answer to either of these questions. I first noticed that I was ill when I was in my twenties, I can't say it started on a day like this, because, I am unsure of how it started it just came up on me, I suppose like a slow wave in the sea gathering speed and depth and washing over me, just like each bad episode has happened it creeps up slowly as I have got further down.

I haven't usually known about them until I am too deep in and then have to take time off work, I have known so many people like this.

Over the years I have tried to work out where my bouts of this illness start so that I can balance my life, but, I haven't until this time, I realised where I was going because, I could feel the glass bowl slowly coming down over me.

I have had it every time I get out of one relationship to the next, I was hoping that it wasn't going to happen, what I didn't realise was that every time I moved out of a relationship it was just suppressed with happiness to get out of it and the stages started before I was out of it, it just took time for me to realise and before it was too late I am there.

This time wasn't any different, I had been in and out of depression for a long time, I had seen a counsellor twice if not three times within 6 years and my best girlfriend would know the difference, she has come to know the signs of my depression of me pushing people especially friends away, being stuck inside all the time, staying up until all hours and still being able to get up at silly times, so no sleep at all, I would sit up writing, not being able to concentrate on tv but, listening to music (not a bad thing).

What I didn't realise until this time was that every time I have had a bout of this illness was that I only scratched the surface in fact barely scratched the surface, every time I felt better I would ignore it and I couldn't get to what was really making me feel this way.

This time I supported someone I love through his own breakdown getting to the real reasons of what has happened to make him breakdown and he has worked through them, so when he started to see what was happening to me he held me and supported me until I finally said to him what was going on even though he said he could see the difference and knew.

You see the difference this time was when I had sat down and talked to him about his problem a few months before, I was scared and worried that I was going to go down the same path so I kept trying to tell myself even though I could feel it that it wasn't happening, we got through Christmas with my painted smile and my paranoia, I started a new contract so I didn't have to drive so far because of my DVT from before Christmas, this hadn't helped, but, slowly I started to deteriorate as my partner, he started to get better.

When I became ill I was finding it harder and harder to be with people outside of work, as I worked it felt like I was being normal, when I got home there was a sense of relief. I got myself through an interview for another contract which I thought was going to help me. It did, I suddenly realised after a month or two how bad I really was.

What I am trying to tell you, is it doesn't matter how happy you are or how stable you think you are it can just happen unless you start talking to someone. To be honest having the strength in my new partner, a new stronger man, someone who actually knows me and understands depression my illness has helped me to keep going.

Someone might now put their hand up and say how can you work and have this illness? I have struggled and I am still struggling with it. I have just started to realise that along with helping my partner with the last of his breakdown and helping him with his mum I would like to work a four day week having three days at the weekend, which I find does help and is refreshing for a Monday morning at the moment I am waiting for approval of this application. If she was to hear this and I actually owned up to why I am not sure how my manager would feel, perhaps I should give her this post as my application.

I want to be able to say after this contract or even this what will hopefully be my last and final bout of this illness that I got through this whilst working. If it wasn't for this blog and being able to talk to some of my new and one of my old friends I wouldn't have been able to do this.

Having someone to talk to has helped a lot, having someone to encourage me and nudge me to do things, someone who supports me in all that I do telling me when things made sense and when they didn't, supporting me in everything, doing some new things as well and compromising with different things has helped extremely and lastly to allow me to cry for no reason.

I have been fortunate and lucky to find someone like this whilst allowing me to talk to others through my blog or on different forums. He believes in me and that can't be anything but, the greatest feeling for someone who is a depression sufferer, sometimes it has it's downfalls, but, then he picks me up and holds me when it goes wrong, telling me to try again or saying that you are here for something, you were saved twice in your lifetime.

I am a human being, things can go wrong. I write because I love writing, because I feel this is the only way I can explain what I have gone through in my illness, I am not a speaker by nature(I have tried that by trying to train as a Methodist Preacher), it helps me to get my thoughts out.

One day I will see more people with depression and other mental health illness in work because employers have heard what is being said by the experts, the ones who have experienced the working environment without someone to help them.

One day I will see others understand what this illness is, that it isn't imaginary as I have experienced, that it isn't a joke, it isn't something to be pushed aside as you may or may not realise one day.

I will see the day when all this silence becomes talking about Mental Health Illnesses, when we can talk openly about our emotions and the pain of the past to be able to get to somewhere without fighting and challenging everything.

There are enough challenges in our lives without fighting or arguing over what is normal and what isn't. We were all put here for a reason, we just want to be seen for what it is so that we can survive.

My name is Susan Bell, I am a writer who lives with depression I will get past this or find a way to manage it better and will keep fighting the deafening silence around me.

Thank you for reading about me today.

Sunday, 30th June 2013 - A Chance!

As you can see I am on a high, a good place, this doesn't mean things are better and the pain has gone away it just means I have had help from some pretty amazing people who have seen me for me and past the pain I hide inside with the smile on the outside, the hurt is still there, the pain is still hurting but, this will get better:-

Tonight,
I simply breathe
Breath the sigh of relief
Relief that I have been given
Given another chance in life

A Chance in life
For me to sit
Sit and look around
Look around at the amazing
Amazing people around
People who are great company

Thank you
For giving me the time
Time to watch
Watch the wonders
Wonders that are around

Around the corner
The corner of each step
Each step new or old
New or old parts of my life
The life I have which has changed

As each change is made
Each step I take
The path I make
Is so different
In each and every way
Each and every day

For each and every one of those days
I will have something new
Something new to help me
Help me get past the old
Old pain and history

The pain and history of my life
My life which has helped me
Helped me to get here
Here is where I want to be
Wanting to be here with you

You my new friends
New friends and old friends
Some place here
Old place there
This is my life

My life wouldn't be mine
Mine to live
If I wasn't given another chance
Ones Chance to change
Change things for the better

That is what my life will begin to be for the better!

Epilogue

My name is Roger, I'm Susie's partner and I have suffered from mental health issues for at least two years which I'm now able to recognise.

It was shortly after I met Susie things came to a head and I had a breakdown, due to the pressures of family issues, work and ill health. However it took me a further three months to admit I had a problem and seek the help I needed to start my road to recovery.

Nine months later, and with Susie's, friends', and my family's help, and of course many hours of telephone and face to face counselling I finally feel there is light at the end of the tunnel.

Once I accepted I did have a breakdown, it was hard to accept the fact I needed to go on antidepressants as this felt like a further failure, however please know they are not a weakness but a vital tool to keep your reserves up whilst you fight the illness.

The next hardest thing for me was to talk to someone, not through being ashamed; I just couldn't put how I was feeling into words, this was upsetting to those who loved me and difficult for them to understand. Once I found my voice again it was still difficult to admit how I was feeling, but by taking small steps, setting goals, and accepting you will have good and bad days you can move forward.

As I was unable to work due to other medical problems I knew I had to find something to concentrate on, so for me it was a combination of gardening and helping Susie with her blog and this book, which stopped me from dwelling on things, whilst explaining how I was feeling to her as I was able to slowly open up.

One of the biggest steps I took towards my road to recovery was admitting to my friends I had a mental health issue, some ran a mile others didn't know what to say, but most of my friends just simply said we are here if you need us, and that was all I needed to hear.

Looking ahead I know I still have some way to go, my confidence is still low and I still suffer from anxiety problems but I will beat this and breakdown some of the stigma walls in the process.

Finally all I can stay is if you suffer from mental health issues please stay strong you are not alone, or if you know someone who is suffering, don't shy away from them, you can't catch the illness, ask them how they are, support them, be a friend, which is exactly what I'm doing with Susie now as she comes to terms with her depression and seeks the help she needs to travel that road to recovery as I am.

List of Mental Health Organisations

UK

Mind
Website: www.mind.org.uk
Info line : 0300 123 3393
Email: contact@mind.org.uk

Time To Change
Led by Mind & Rethink Mental Illness
Website: www.time-to-change.org.uk
Email: info@time-to-change.org.uk

Rethink Mental Illness
Website: www.rethink.org
Info line : 0300 5000 927
Email   : advice@rethink.org or info@rethink.org

SANE
Website: www.sane.org.uk
Helpline: 0845 767 8000
Email   : From their website

USA

Mental Health America
Website: www.mentalhealthamerica.net
Helpline: 1-800-273-TALK(8255) - USA dial
Email   : info@mentalhealthamerica.net

Australia

Mental Health Association Australia
Website: www.mentalhealth.org.au
Helpline : 1300 729 686 - Australia dial
Email   : info@mentalhealth.org.au

Canada

Canadian Mental Health Association
Website: http://www.cmha.ca/
Helpline: Please find in your own Provence on www.cmha.ca/get-involved/find-your-cmha
Email   : Please find in your own Provence on www.cmha.ca/get-involved/find-your-cmha

Some of the above organisations have their own forums. For instance Mind is Elefriends of which 50 pence for every book sold is being donated to as they it is a very good forum for those with Mental Health Illnesses.

Facebook Pages

Kissing Stigma Goodbye
I'm OK
Mental Illness Is Hidden
Heartily Mindful
Footsteps to Mental Health
I am Not My Illness

There are a lot more that are community mental health pages who are not medical staff, however their experience as you have heard from Sara Breidenstein in the Preface of my book, please look on them as there is a wide range of different pages, if I went on to talk about them we would be in a few months when my next book would be due.

Printed in Great Britain
by Amazon